DREAMLAND

DREAMLAND

AMERICA AT THE DAWN OF THE TWENTIETH CENTURY

MICHAEL LESY

THE NEW PRESS ∞ NEW YORK

Published in the United States by The New Press, New York
Distributed by W.W. Norton & Company, Inc., New York

The New Press was established in 1990 as a not-for-profit alternative
to the large, commercial publishing houses currently dominating the
book publishing industry. The New Press operates in the public interest
rather than for private gain, and is committed to publishing, in innovative
ways, works of educational, cultural, and community value that might
not normally be commercially viable. The New Press's offices are located
at the City University of New York

Book design by Smyth and Whiteside of BAD
Production management by Kim Waymer
Printed in the United States of America
9 8 7 6 5 4 3 2 1

After such knowledge, what forgiveness? Think now
History has many cunning passages, contrived corridors
And issues, deceives with whispering ambitions,
Guides us by vanities. Think now
She gives when our attention is distracted
And what she gives, give with such supple confusions
That the giving famishes the craving. Gives too late
What's not believed in, or if still believed,
In memory only, reconsidered passion. Gives too soon
Into weak hands, what's thought can be dispensed with
Till the refusal propagates a fear. Think
Neither fear nor courage saves us. Unnatural vices
Are fathered by our heroism. Virtues
Are forced upon us by our impudent crimes.
These tears are shaken from the wrath-bearing tree.

— T. S. Eliot, Gerontion (1920)

CONTENTS

ACKNOWLEDGMENTS

MY THANKS TO ANDRÉ SCHIFFRIN, director of The New Press, for believing enough in this project to publish it, and to Gregory Prince, president of Hampshire College, for believing in it enough to support it. Their cordiality and collaboration made was only possible into something real.

Roger Straus III, my friend and, on several occasions, my co-conspirator, provided technical and tactical advice that kept me sane. In Washington, Bryan Wilkins, Catherine Grayson, and their children, William, Torrey, and Emily, gave me shelter, through many storms, through many seasons. In Amherst, Jeff Sharlet and Kio Stark offered critical advice and openhearted friendship during crucial moments in the work. Molly Chilson, Ingrid Ducmanis, Amy Ennis, Jennifer Ewing, and Kevin Morrison, once students and now friends, provided a range of insight and support throughout the undertaking. Jacqueline Hayden, associate professor of photography at Hampshire College, and Steven Weisler, professor of linguistics at Hampshire told me what they thought and what they felt about the project in ways only true friends can. Throughout it all my wife, Elizabeth, my daughter, Nadia, and my son, Alex tolerated my absences and my obsessions.

I owe thanks, in Denver to Eric Paddock, curator of photography, at the Colorado Historical Society, for his knowledge, friendship, and support; to Jay DiLorenzo, staff photographer, and Michael "Spyder" Ren, assistant photographer, for their professional services; and to Barbara Foley, at the Stephen Hart Library of the Society and Rebecca Lintz, assistant director of collection services at the Society, for their careful attention to detail.

In Amherst, I am indebted to Nancy Kelley, executive assistant, Mary Costello, administrative assistant, and Yaniris Fernandez, assistant, all in the President's office at Hampshire College, for their professionalism and patience; to Lenore Bowen, administrative assistant, and Yen Chun Mao, administrative secretary, both in the office of the School of Cultural Studies and Cognitive Science, Hampshire College, for their good-natured assistance, and to Nancy Dobosz, director of purchasing, for her dispatch.

I offer my thanks, in Washington, to Mary Isom, director of prints and photographs, Reading Room, Library of Congress, for her diplomacy, and to Carol Johnson, assistant curator of photography, at the Library, for her hands-on help and advice. In the photographic section of the Library, Eva Shade, assistant head of that section, provided a level of technical excellence that far exceeded anything available in the private sector. ➤

ALMOST ONE HUNDRED YEARS AGO, at the very edge of the twentieth century, William Henry Jackson and a rich man from Detroit named William Livingstone formed a partnership that lasted twenty-five years. Jackson, whose western landscapes every photographer knows, owned an astonishing collection of negatives, his own and others'; Livingstone had acquired the rights to a Swiss color photolithographic process. The result was mass-produced, colored images—not mechanically reproduced artists' renderings, but brilliantly inked, precisely registered photolithographs that mimed the sensual clarity of the world.

Together with another man (a photographer named Edwin Husher) Jackson and Livingstone in 1898 formed the Detroit Publishing Company. Their company made and sold seven million images a year—color postcards, panoramas, and slides—distributing them worldwide: over the counter at resorts and tourist attractions, by mail order, and through its own outlets in cities like New York, Boston, and Los Angeles. In 1902, Jackson led a Detroit Publishing Company crew of photographers across the country in a specially equipped railroad car, making photographs as they went, an eerie variation on the federally sponsored Hayden Surveys, in which Jackson had participated during the 1870s. In 1924, having suffered through the labor and supply rationing of World War I, the Detroit Publishing Company went bankrupt. It had been one of the largest and most active publishers of photographic views in America.

Travelers bought the company's postcards just as travelers buy postcards now, but they also bought them in boxed sets, which the company's 1901 catalog described as "book-like in appearance, suitable for library shelves." Public schools bought sets of the company's lantern slides. Municipal governments, civic associations, and public libraries bought their panoramas—"up to 150 inches in length. In larger sizes they are very impressive"—and displayed them in their offices and reading rooms. Collectors bought their hand-colored prints, assured by the company's catalog that "this work has a character of its own...producing most beautiful and dainty effects that never fail to awaken unusual admiration."

From 1898 until the copyright laws changed in 1909, Detroit Publishing dutifully deposited an example of every "scenic view" it produced in the Library of Congress. Twelve years after the company went out of business, its entire file of negatives and prints, by then comprising images made in every state in the Union by dozens of company photographers, was purchased by the Edison Institute in Dearborn; ten years after that, the Institute shipped every one of the company's negatives to the Colorado

State Historical Society in Denver, William Henry Jackson's home town. The State Historical Society kept every negative made west of the Mississippi. Everything else— twentieth-century American cities and towns, factories and parks, people and landscapes— was sent to the Library of Congress. Which is where I first saw them, back in 1984.

For the past twelve years, as this country skids into the twenty-first century, I've been looking at these images. I've been trying to understand why, every time I see them, every time I study them, I feel both like a man who's just seen the woman he once loved and like a diver who's just run out of air.

One reason is the very breadth of the collection: cityscapes and quiet little towns, central parks and endless prairies, California orange groves and Kansas City stockyards, depots and mines, coal breakers and steel mills, tenants picking cotton in Mississippi and dandies striding across Herald Square, rich men in Florida and newsboys in Indianapolis, boardrooms in New York and dusty lanes in the Berkshires, ore boats in Cleveland and iron mines in Birmingham, suspension bridges, dread-noughts, steel-beamed skyscrapers, electric trolleys, and bicycles and wagons passed by the first automobiles—all the wonders and contradictions of the early twentieth century are arrayed in miniature, image after image, beating past the eyes like the strokes of a metronome.

In these pictures, nature has been reduced to vistas seen on vacation, wit-nessed by solitary figures: a man in a tweed suit, knees drawn up, seated on a boulder, overlooking a valley; or a pair of women in shirtwaists, holding hands, high on a bluff, gazing at a river, or a lone fisherman, wearing a suit vest and a straw hat, resting on his oars, framed by the shores of a lake.

The marvels recorded by the company's photographs aren't nature's but man's: gigantic mills rise like Permian cliffs along the banks of a river in Pennsylvania; ten-story ore docks, made of first-growth timber, stretch like promontories into Lake Superior, and Great Lakes ore boats loom in shipyards like monstrous whales left behind by the waters of the Flood. In the vast truss-roofed train stations of great cities, the parallel lines of track converge to infinity; at the end of avenues, twenty-story office buildings rise as stark as buttes from a plain; and in shopping arcades, where the shop windows sparkle, crowds saunter past and then recede like reflections at the bottom of a well.

The man-made world as it appears in these pictures is not only grand but balanced, graceful, and harmonious, a world whose tacit virtues have to do with the luxury of uncluttered and expansive public space—a world of air, clear light, mannered civility, and well-tended order, in which even the crowds, strolling through parks or passing public squares or milling along the shore, are so modest in size and so comfortably disposed as to appear choreographed.

It is the world we have lost: its safety, its self-confidence, its vigor, its serenity, its possibilities—its space. Parts of every city the Detroit Publishing Company photographed are now slag heaps and war zones; the great mills have been cut apart, sold as scrap, and made into toasters; the most distant places drone with engine noise and chatter. The only vistas now available illustrate auto commercials; the most commonly experienced reveries are now achieved behind locked doors.

Of course the world as reproduced by the company was neither as harmonious nor as grand as it appeared. Absent were the tenements and airless rooms, the clattering machines and clock-driven repetitions, the epidemics, adulterated food, impoverishments, strikes, brutalities, and corruption that everyone from the muckrakers to such conservative social philosophers as George Beard and Max Nordau identified as the great toxins of "modern" life. The office buildings, bridges, mills, and factories that looked so imposing in the pictures appeared so only because they stood alone like pieces on a game board: the Flatiron Building, the Times Building, and the elevated tracks towered above a city skyline that reached only ten stories. There were other absences as well: when workers appeared, they either posed with their tools or bent to docile work or were seen from a distance, solitary figures crossing broken ground or clustered near structures that dwarfed them. Native Americans—Crows, Ojibwas, Zunis, and Navajos—appeared as exotics or curiosities; African Americans, complete with racist captions, were cast as anecdotes ("Seden come 'Leben") or entertainment ("Happy as the Day is Long").

Still, when the company's cameras came close enough to look into the eyes of stevedores or iron workers or seamen or miners or cowboys, these men looked back from faces that, seen today, are authentically different from the faces of people now alive. The glances of these men, long dead, give evidence of a time both similar and not at all like ours—our present resembling that past the way a blind beggar, in some fairy tale, might declare that once he had been king. One impulse is not to believe the man, to ridicule him, to deny—even after excuses and explanations and a tiresome recitation of near fatal mistakes—that such an outcast had once ruled the land. But the people in these pictures—the ones who crossed streets or strolled through parks or rode the trolleys or played in the surf—none of them were fictions nor were the worlds they inhabited within each picture frame. The customers who for twenty-five years bought the postcards were no fools—they knew the difference between things real and things imagined. The company wasn't photographing Mars or Atlantis or the Emerald City; the world it reproduced might not have been the whole truth, but it was a recognizable one.

What we now know to be true we have learned only because of the passage of time: the arrow of progress that these people—our ancestors—shot into the air has landed in our backs. The moment when these pictures were made was like the instant—strangely painless—after a deep clean, knife wound. All the underground treasures—the oil, the ore, the coal, and the stone—were being dug up from the earth, and all the toxins we now live with were being let loose.

Detroit Publishing sold images of affirmation. Our ancestors bought, sent, and kept them as testaments and reminders: "We were here; it was remarkable; see what we saw." One hundred years later, we see things differently. We think their pictures are proud, handsome, and beautiful, but we also understand that inside every image of power and certainly was not just diminution and decay, but the very cause of that decay: a copper smelter in Michigan, built in a pasture, cows in the foreground, a brick chimney, behind black smoke billowing into a clear sky. "Stop!" we want to say. "Wait!" we want to say. But our ancestors didn't stop, and because they didn't, we exist as we do today.

We can respond to the images in a variety of ways, seeing them as foolish, as naive, even as tragic. Or we can understand them as images of possibility, not as models to reconstruct what was, but as reminders of a state of hope—that, knowing all we know, we might, in some fashion, be able to make the world seem whole again. ➥

SOME FACTS

IN 1900, 76 MILLION PEOPLE INHABITED the United States and its Territories—Territories that included Arizona and Oklahoma, as well as Alaska and Hawaii in 1893, annexed two years before, after an American-backed coup ousted the island's queen. Cuba and the Philippines were still occupied by American forces following the naval defeat of Spain in the "glorious little war" of 1898. American military commissioners ruled Cuba; American Army forces, led by a Civil War hero, fought Philippine nationalist guerrillas who believed the destruction of the Spanish fleet entitled them to sovereignty. American national interests understood that event differently: the Philippines were to be a steppingstone to the China Market.

Forty percent of Americans lived in cities and towns; sixty percent lived in the countryside, in villages and on farms. New York was the largest city in the country with a population of 3.4 million, followed by Chicago,

with 1.7, and Philadelphia, with 1.3. The total population of Los Angeles was 103,000. Of a total workforce of 29 million people, 11 million worked the land on 6 million farms; six million worked in mills and factories, another 3 million waited on customers or worked as domestics. Trade, banking, and real estate occupied 2.7 million people; two million others worked for the railroads and the rarely public utilities. Nearly 2 million men worked construction; roughly 800,000 worked as miners; another 200,000 worked as lumberjacks and fishermen. In 1900, there were 220,000 blacksmiths and 7,000 newsboys.

In 1900, white men could expect to live 46 years; white women, 48. Non-whites had an average life expectancy of 33 years. Pneumonia, tuberculosis, and influenza killed most of the people. Coronary, circulatory, and renal failure killed nearly as many. Cancer, as a primary cause of death, was a distant fourth, behind gastrointestinal illnesses such as

dysentery. Diphtheria, typhoid, malaria, measles, and whooping cough killed large numbers of children and adults. In all the United States, in 1900, there were only 131,000 doctors and 12,000 nurses.

In that same year, less than 250,000 people attended college. Nonetheless, nearly 90 percent of the population was considered literate. One result was that there were 2000 daily papers, with a combined circulation of 15 million copies. By 1913, more than 500 foreign language papers had been added to that number—papers printed in 29 different languages, in 35 of the 48 states.

By 1910, 23 million Americans identified themselves as the children of foreign or mixed parentage. Twenty percent of them claimed German ancestry; 13 percent said they were of Irish descent. In 1900, 8.8 million African-Americans were counted in the census. Nearly 55 percent of them lived on farms; the great majority of these farmers were tenants who owned little more than their ability to work. That same census counted almost 250,000 Native Americans, many living in a zone called Indian Territory, later annexed to Oklahoma.

In 1900, nearly 500,000 immigrants entered the United States. By 1905, that number had doubled. Of those million, more than a quarter came from the Austrio-Hungarian Empire—Czechs, Slavs, Serbs, Croatians, Austrians, and Hungarians. Another 200,000 came from Poland, Lithuania, and Russia. Many of those were Jews. In 1912, more than 150,000 Italians entered the United States. Most of them were from southern Italy; the greatest number from Campania, Calabria, and Sicily.

The owners of mines and factories hired these immigrants in large numbers and paid them as little as they could. In 1910, more than 50 percent of the men who worked in the country's iron and steel mills were immigrants.

In 1910, the annual minimum subsistence wage was calculated to be $750. The average wage paid to immigrants was $400 less than that. In Pueblo, Colorado, the Pueblo Steel Works employed nearly 3,000 men. More than 75 percent of them were foreign born—Mexicans and Italians, Slavs, Greeks, Austrians, and Japanese.

In 1910, half the population of Utah, Montana, the Dakotas, Minnesota, Wisconsin, Michigan, and Illinois were immigrants, drawn to the factories, mines, and logging camps of those states. Public schools were the places where the children of these men who worked for half wages became Americans. In 1910, one-quarter of the 18 million students enrolled in public schools were the offspring of immigrants.

In 1910, the ten largest corporations in the United States included a leather company, a shipping company, a sugar company, a meat company, a tobacco company, and a copper company. Of those ten giant corporations, U.S. Steel and Standard Oil of New Jersey were the largest. Of those ten, only the Pullman Company and International Harvester built machines. In the entire United States in 1900, there were only 8,000 automobiles and less than 1.3 million telephones. The telegraph carried messages; railroads carried freight and passengers; trollies and horses transported people. In 1900, people wrote each other letters and sent each other postcards. ◄

DREAMLAND

Crowds and Solitaries

Massive Forms and Enormous Spaces

70770. COLONIAL ARCADE CLEVELAND O.

1900

CORPORATIONS, CLASS CONFLICT, AND CURRENCY

One hundred thousand anthracite coal miners went on strike. The strike lasted six weeks. By then the price of coal had risen 500 percent in New York City.

Congress voted to establish gold as the standard for U.S. currency. Farmers, small businessmen, and debtors, large and small, led by the Populist Democrat William Jennings Bryan, continued to agitate for the free coinage of silver, easy credit, and federal regulation of the railroads. Many of them believed there was an international conspiracy between Jewish bankers and Wall Street financiers.

Carnegie Steel was incorporated in New Jersey. It became the seventh largest corporation in the United States.

POLITICS

William Goebel, the Democratic reform candidate for governor of Kentucky, was assassinated as soon as he was elected. Political factions in the state prepared for a civil war.

The Republican Party, under the control of Cleveland political boss Mark Hanna, nominated William McKinley for reelection as president. The party selected Theodore Roosevelt, the governor of New York, as vice president.

The Democrats nominated William Jennings Bryan for president. They had done the same thing in 1896.

The Social Democratic Party nominated Eugene V. Debs. In 1894, Debs had been jailed for leading his union—the American Railway Union—in a strike against the Pullman Company. A court injunction and federal troops ended that strike.

McKinley won in November. The popular vote was McKinley, 7.2 million; Bryan, 6.3 million; Social Democrats, Populists, and Prohibitionists, combined, 350,000.

FOREIGN POLICY

Congress declared Hawaii to be a United States territory.

General Arthur McArthur, American military governor of the Philippines, proclaimed amnesty for Philippine nationalist insurgents. Meanwhile, he sent troops to capture their leader, Emilio Aguinaldo.

Two thousand U.S. Marines, along with troops from Great Britain, France, Germany, Russia, and Japan entered Peking, liberated the British legation, and ended the nationalist Chinese Boxer Rebellion. The United States used the occasion to promote its Open Door policy, first proclaimed by Secretary of State John Hay the year before. Hay's Open Door promulgated a new American imperial economic policy: the China market and all foreign markets were to be open to anyone who could compete for them. Control of markets, not colonies, became a new goal of U.S. foreign policy.

In Cuba, Walter Reed and three other physicians began the research to find the cause—and cure—of Yellow Fever.

TECHNOLOGY AND MANUFACTURING

Wilbur and Orville Wright flew their first full-scale glider at Kitty Hawk.

The Olds Company opened its first automobile assembly plant in Detroit. Workers built one car at a time, from parts made by other manufacturers. By the end of the plant's second year, Olds was producing four cars a day.

Eastman Kodak sold its first Brownie box camera. Low cost, ease of use, and flexible film produced the mass phenomenon of the snapshot.

CITYSCAPES

Boston's Symphony Hall, designed
by the firm of McKim, Mead, and
White, opened to the public. The firm—
which had already designed the Boston
Public Library and the Columbia
University campus—went on to
design the Pierpont Morgan Library,
Pennsylvania Station, and dozens
of private clubs, museums, banks, post
offices, and commercial buildings—
all in the grand Renaissance style
espoused by the Ecole des Beaux-Arts.

BOOKS, SONGS, AND EVENTS

Doubleday, Page, and Company published Theodore Dreiser's first novel,
Sister Carrie. The company abandoned
the book once Mrs. Doubleday and her
husband realized how vulgar and
immoral Dreiser's story was.

Also published: L. Frank Baum's
The Wizard of Oz, Theodore Roosevelt's
The Strenuous Life, and Jack London's
Yukon stories, *The Son of the Wolf*.

The year's most popular song was
"Good-bye Dolly Gray," a war song
about a soldier leaving for the
Philippines. Also popular: "Strike Up
the Band—Here Comes a Sailor" and
"A Bird in a Gilded Cage."

In Vaughan, Mississippi, an Illinois
Central Railway engineer named John
Luther Jones—known as Casey—
died at the throttle of his express train.
Jones died trying to slow his train before
it crashed into the rear of another. His
death saved his passengers' lives and
made him a hero.

Baseball's American League declared
itself a major league, elbowed its way
into National League cities, and convinced players to abandon its rival. The
American League had its origin, twenty
years earlier, in an association that had
prospered by playing ball on Sunday
and selling beer to its fans.

DISASTERS

A hurricane with 120-mile-an-hour
winds followed by a tidal wave swept
over Galveston, Texas, and killed 5,000
people. Stereographic "view" companies
sent photographic crews to record the
disaster and sell pictures of it to the public.

In Hoboken, New Jersey, a fire
destroyed the docks of two ocean steamship companies, burned down two ocean
liners, and incinerated 326 people.

A mine explosion in Scofield, Utah,
killed 200 men.

013391. RIVERSIDE PARK, NEW YORK.

COPR. DETROIT PHOTOGRAPHIC CO.

019272. A DRIVEWAY IN EDEN PARK, CINCINNATI, OHIO.

D34070. SOUTH STATION, BOSTON, MASS.

DETROIT PUBLISHING CO.

1901

POLITICS, FOREIGN, AND DOMESTIC

The same month William McKinley was sworn in for his second term, U.S. forces in the Philippines captured Emilio Aguinaldo, the Philippine guerrilla leader. Aguinaldo's capture ended the three-year insurrection against U.S. occupation.

Six months later, an anarchist shot and killed President McKinley at the Pan-American Exposition in Buffalo— an exposition meant to celebrate American preeminence in the hemisphere.

Four days before McKinley died, Theodore Roosevelt, his vice president, had given a speech at a state fair in Minnesota advocating a two-ocean navy to enforce the Monroe Doctrine. "Speak softly and carry a big stick," Roosevelt said. Mark Hanna, the Republican power broker, referred to Roosevelt as "that damned cowboy." Earlier in the year, Congress had attached an amendment to an army appropriations bill that made Cuba a virtual U.S. protectorate. The Platt Amendment, as it was called, remained in place for the next thirty-four years.

One month after Roosevelt became president (at the time, the youngest in United States history), he invited the African American educator Booker T. Washington to have dinner with him in the White House. It was the first time a prominent African American had ever dined with a president. Southern Democrats were appalled.

TRUSTS, RAW MATERIALS, AND THE STOCK MARKET

Andrew Carnegie retired from the steel business by selling everything he owned to financier J. Pierpont Morgan. Morgan formed a new corporation—U.S. Steel— by combining Carnegie's holdings with the Mesabi Range iron mines owned by John D. Rockefeller. The result was a billion-dollar corporation—the first in American history—that produced 60 percent of all the iron and steel made in the United States.

Meanwhile, Meyer Guggenheim and his sons extended the operations of ASARCO, their Copper Trust. ASARCO owned copper, tin, and nitrate mines in Bolivia and Chile, gold mines in Alaska, and diamond mines, copper mines, and rubber plantations in the Belgian Congo.

In Texas, the Spindletop gusher in the Beaumont field made the Gulf Oil Company (and its principal investor, the Pittsburgh banker Andrew Mellon) the country's first rival to John D. Rockefeller's Standard Oil. For the next twenty years, the United States would produce two-thirds of the world's oil.

In Milwaukee, the Johns Manville Company began to import asbestos from Canada. The company would become the largest manufacturer of insulation in the world.

An Indiana banker named Daniel Reed merged 175 U.S. can companies to form a trust called American Can. The trust manufactured 90 percent of all tin-plated steel cans made in the United States.

On Wall Street, stock manipulations by investors fighting for control of the Northern Pacific Railroad, owned by J. P. Morgan and James Hill, resulted in a Panic. The investors' takeover efforts failed, but not before brokerage houses dumped stock to cover their short positions in Northern Pacific holdings. The result was a general collapse in prices.

1901

MANUFACTURING, RESEARCH, AND TECHNOLOGY

In Detroit, Henry Ford was hired as an experimental engineer by the Detroit Auto Company.

In Lansing, Michigan, Ransom Olds built a new factory financed by Michigan lumber and copper money. By 1904, it was producing 500 cars a year.

In Cleveland, the American Multigraph Company began to manufacture machines that could print multiple copies from handwritten or typewritten stencils.

In Baltimore, a research team funded by Armor & Company isolated adrenaline, the first ductless gland secretion ever isolated in a laboratory.

In Newfoundland, the inventor Guglielmo Marconi heard the first Morse code transmission ever sent by radio waves across the Atlantic.

In Havana, the U.S. Yellow Fever Commission reported experiments that proved the disease was transmitted by a variety of mosquito. Two American researchers died making the discovery.

GOOD DEEDS, BOOKS, AND SONGS

Andrew Carnegie began a twenty-year career of philanthropy. By the time he died, he'd given away $350 million. One of his first gifts was $5 million to the New York Public Library.

Frank Norris wrote *The Octopus* about the fight of California wheat farmers against the Southern Pacific Railroad. *The Octopus* was to be the first of a trilogy of exposés about the power of railroads and trusts. Norris died before he could complete all three volumes. In 1903, *The Pit*—about Chicago wheat speculators—was published posthumously.

Also published: *The Making of an American* by Jacob Riis, the photographer and reformer, and Booker T. Washington's *Up from Slavery*.

Popular songs included "Boola Boola," written by a Yale student, and "I Love You Truly."

DISASTERS AND FOLLIES

In Jacksonville, Florida, a fire destroyed 1,700 buildings and left 10,000 people homeless.

In the Philippines, white rice, introduced into the diet by U.S. occupation forces, produced an epidemic of beriberi.

20

EORGETOWN. COL.
W.H.J.

GRANDE RESTAURANT
TER AND CHOP HOUSE.

LIQUORS CIGARS.

04228 MAIN ST. UPPER CREEDE.

017341. GOVERNMENT SQUARE, CINCINNATI, O.   DETROIT PHOTOGRAPHIC Co.

0-217. DURANGO FROM THE RESERVOIR.

016254. GAGNON MINE, BUTTE, MONTANA.

Constructions and Erections

Towers, Wedges, Wombs, and Vanishing Points

COPR. DETROIT PHOTOGRAPHIC CO.

1902

FOREIGN AND DOMESTIC POLICY

France's failed Panama Canal Company, unable to overcome a combination of malaria, yellow fever, and impossible terrain, offered to sell its interests to the United States for $40 million, a little more than one-third its original asking price. The U.S. Isthmian Canal Commission recommended the Panama route to President Roosevelt. The commission's recommendation was influenced by a New York lawyer named William Cromwell and a French engineer named Phillipe Bunau-Varilla. Cromwell had made a $60,000 contribution to the Republican Party to convince Mark Hanna to lobby for the Panamanian route. In 1903, following a revolt against Colombia, planned by Bunau-Vanilla and engineered by the United States, Bunau-Varilla became Panama's first ambassador to the United States.

Six months after the commission made its recommendation, Congress voted to authorize the president to accept France's offer, arrange terms with the government of Colombia, and begin construction of an Isthmian canal.

The same month Congress authorized the canal, it passed a reclamation act, beginning a massive program of dam building and irrigation in sixteen Western states.

On Independence Day, President Roosevelt declared the Philippine Insurrection to be ended. Congress declared the people of the Philippines to be United States territorial citizens. Two months earlier, Cuba had declared itself a republic—under U.S. protection.

TRUSTS AND CLASS CONFLICT

Cyrus McCormick, Jr., was persuaded by J. P. Morgan to underwrite a trust that merged four major harvesting machine manufacturers. The new company, called International Harvester, controlled 85 percent of all reaper production in the United States. The company became the sixth largest corporation in the country.

In the spring, 147,000 anthracite miners went on strike for higher wages and union recognition. The strike lasted five months and nearly crippled the country. By September, the price of coal in New York City had risen from $5 to $14 a ton. Mobs of western miners seized coal cars headed east. By October, the price of a ton of coal had risen to $30. President Roosevelt intervened, and the result was higher wages but no union recognition.

A month after the strike ended, a mine owner in Telluride, Colorado, was assassinated in his home. The governor of Colorado sent National Guard troops to fight the Western Federation of Miners.

In *McClure's* Magazine, the journalist Ida Tarbell began a series of exposés that later became a book, *The History of Standard Oil*. Tarbell's research revealed that J. D. Rockefeller controlled 90 percent of all domestic oil refining.

1902

MANUFACTURING, RESEARCH, AND TECHNOLOGY

Three new motor cars (all made in Indiana) were sold to the public for the first time. One—the Studebaker—ran on batteries. Another—the Marmon—was powered by an air-cooled, overhead valve engine.

In Detroit, Henry Ford's "999" race car set a track record of sixty mph.

At Kitty Hawk, the Wright Brothers' third glider made nearly 1,000 flights, some of more than 600 feet.

BUSINESS AND MARKETING

J. C. Penney and his wife opened their first store in Kenmore, Wyoming.

In North Carolina, a pharmacist named Caleb Bradham closed his drugstore so he could devote himself to his new enterprise: the Pepsi-Cola Company.

In Easton, Pennsylvania, the family firm of Benny and Smith began to make Crayola Brand crayons.

In Brooklyn, a Russian American candy store owner and his wife stitched together the first Teddy Bear. They'd been inspired by a cartoon of the President refusing to shoot a mother bear while on a hunting trip in Mississippi.

The first Animal Crackers were marketed by the National Biscuit Company. The crackers were packed in a little box that could be hung from the family Christmas tree. National Biscuit made 70 percent of all crackers and cookies sold in the United States.

In Hawaii, James Dole bought a 12,000-acre plantation, planted it with pineapples, and began the Hawaiian Pineapple Company.

CITYSCAPES

In New York, the twenty-story, steel-framed Flatiron Building was completed. It was designed by the Chicago architect Daniel Burnham.

In Washington, the McMillan Commission released a report calling for the reconstruction of the capital city. It recommended a mall be built, stretching from the White House to the Lincoln Memorial.

CARTOONS, BOOKS, AND SONGS

The cartoon characters Buster Brown and his dog, Tiger, appeared, for the first time, in the *New York Herald*. Buster's maker, Richard Outcault, had drawn Buster's distant cousin, the anti-social Yellow Kid, eight years earlier. Buster was much better dressed and much better behaved.

Owen Wister wrote *The Virginian*. "Smile when you say that" was its most famous line. Also published: Jack London's "To Build a Fire," Helen Keller's *The Story of My Life*, Henry James's *The Wings of the Dove*, and *The Varieties of Religious Experience* by William James, Henry's brother.

Popular songs: "In the Good Old Summer Time" and "Bill Bailey, Won't You Please Come Home." The most popular ragtime song of the year was "Under the Bamboo Tree." Also performed: Jelly Roll Morton's "New Orleans Blues."

EXIT

EQUITABLE LIFE ASSURANCE OFFICES, NEW YORK.

Public Pleasures: Parks and Promenades

Lakes and Sea Shores, Open Air and Clear Water

010843. SHORE DRIVE, LINCOLN PARK, CHICAGO, ILL.

013392. WASHINGTON BRIDGE AND SPEEDWAY, NEW YORK.

013392. WASHINGTON BRIDGE AND SPEEDWAY, NEW YORK.

070177 BAND CONCERT LINCOLN PARK, CHICAGO, ILL.

1903

FOREIGN AND DOMESTIC POLICY

The United States and Colombia signed a treaty leasing a six-mile strip across the Isthmus of Panama. Panama was, at the time, still a province of Colombia. The fee was $10 million plus annual payments. Congress ratified the treaty but stipulated that Colombia surrender all powers in the Canal Zone. The Colombian Senate refused to consent. President Roosevelt responded by calling the Colombians "dagos."

In a Waldorf-Astoria hotel room, the French engineer Bunau-Varilla met with an employee of an Isthmian railroad represented by New York lawyer William Cromwell. Bunau-Varilla gave the railway engineer a flag his wife had made for a new Panamanian republic, as well as a declaration of independence and a constitution.

In November, on the same day that a United States cruiser appeared off the coast of Panama, a revolt broke out against Colombia. The railroad represented by Cromwell refused to transport Colombian troops sent against the insurrection.

Within three days, the United States recognized Panama as a sovereign nation. Two weeks later, Phillipe Bunau-Varilla was appointed Panama's first ambassador to the United States and, in that capacity, signed a version of the treaty originally rejected by the Colombian Senate. J. P. Morgan, serving as the U.S. government's banker, transferred $40 million to the shareholders of the original French Canal Company; William Cromwell was paid $800,000 for legal services rendered.

In New York, Tammany political boss George Washington Plunket gave an interview in which he made a distinction between honest and dishonest graft. He offered himself as an example of honest graft. In his words: "I have seen my opportunities and I took 'em."

In Washington, Congress created a Department of Commerce and Labor whose secretary would have cabinet rank. In 1913, Labor divorced itself from Commerce to form a separate department.

In Florida, President Roosevelt designated Pelican Island as the first National Wildlife Refuge. Also in Florida: the state of Florida acquired title to the Everglades. In 1906, it began to drain them.

TRUSTS, CORPORATIONS, AND COMPANIES

Charles Schwab, former president of Carnegie Steel and, for a brief time, president of U.S. Steel, resigned to buy Bethlehem Steel. He soon merged Bethlehem with a trust he formed called U.S. Shipbuilding. The merger provided Bethlehem with a set of shipbuilding customers and U.S. Ship with a captive source of steel plates.

In Dayton, the founder of the National Cash Register Company gave $1 million to an NCR executive named Thomas J. Watson. Watson was instructed to start a company that would pretend to be NCR's rival but would actually help it gain control of the used cash register business in the United States. Watson's fake company eliminated all rivals in New York City, then moved on to Philadelphia and Chicago. In 1914, Watson became president of the Calculating-Tabulating-Recording Company. Ten years later, the company changed its name to International Business Machines. Watson ran IBM until 1949.

Three giant copper companies merged to form a trust called American Brass. Parties in the merger were Amalgamated Copper (itself controlled by Standard Oil and Anaconda), United Copper (controlled by Montana mine owner Frederick Augustus Henze), and American Smelting and Refining Company (controlled by the Guggenheim family). The growing use of electricity and a steady increase in the number of telephones had created a shortage of copper wire.

In Texas, the oil company known as Texaco brought in its first gusher.

1903

In Detroit, twelve shareholders, including John and Horace Dodge, incorporated the Ford Motor Company. Henry Ford traded designs and patents for stock in the new company. Production began on what Ford called his Model A in an old wagon factory. The first Model A was powered by a two-cylinder, eight-horsepower, chain-drive engine. In ten - months, the company sold 700 cars at $750 each. Seven hundred fifty dollars was equal to one year's minimum wage.

In Derry Church, Pennsylvania, near Harrisburg, Milton Hershey broke ground for a company town and a chocolate factory that soon became the largest such factory in the world.

Michael Owens reengineered an automated glass-blowing machine to produce 2,500 bottles—or electric light bulbs—per hour. Inexpensive, mass-produced light bulbs greatly increased the use of electricity.

Guglielmo Marconi sent the first complete, wireless Morse code message from Wellfleet, Massachusetts, to Cornwall, England.

An undersea cable linked San Francisco with Honolulu and Manila. Using that cable, a message traveled around the world in twelve minutes.

In Kitty Hawk, the Wright Brothers achieved powered flight. Their gasoline powered "Flyer I" flew fifteen feet above the ground for fifty-nine seconds.

MOVIES, SPORTS, BOOKS, AND INFORMATION

The Great Train Robbery, produced in Paterson, New Jersey, by the Edison Company was the first film to tell a story. It lasted twelve minutes.

In the first World Series, the American League's Boston Red Sox beat the National League's Pittsburgh Pirates, 5 games to 3.

Kate Douglas Wiggin's book *Rebecca of Sunnybrook Farm* sold 1 million copies. Also published: Henry James's *The Ambassador*, Frank Norris's *The Pit*, and Jack London's *The Call of the Wild*.

Joseph Pulitzer, publisher of the *New York World*, endowed a school of journalism at Columbia University. Part of his endowment was set aside for yearly prizes to be awarded in his name.

CITYSCAPES

The Williamsburg Bridge, across New York's East River, was completed. It was the first major suspension bridge anchored by steel towers.

In Cincinnati, the sixteen-story Ingall's Building was completed. It was the first skyscraper framed with reinforced concrete instead of steel.

In New York Harbor, Emma Lazarus's poem "The New Colossus," cast in bronze, was set into the base of the Statue of Liberty.

DISASTERS

A fire in the Iroquois Theater in Chicago killed 588 people.

A flood of the Kansas, Missouri and Des Moines Rivers killed 200 people and left 8,000 homeless.

COPYRIGHT·1901·BY·DETROIT·PHOTOGRAPHIC·CO.

019303. FINISH OF A HANDICAP, CRESCENT CITY JOCKY CLUB, NEW ORLEANS, LA.

1904

DOMESTIC POLITICS AND POLICIES

The Republican Party nominated Theodore Roosevelt for president. In the fall, Roosevelt won reelection by 2 million votes, the largest plurality ever received by a candidate. Democratic totals were 5 million; third parties—Populists, Socialists, and Prohibitionists—totaled 776,000.

Earlier in the year, Roosevelt had acquired the reputation of a "trust buster" following a 5 to 4 Supreme Court ruling that the Northern Securities Company, controlled by J. P. Morgan, violated the 1890 Sherman Anti-Trust Act. The case had been prosecuted by Roosevelt's attorney general despite efforts by Morgan to settle the matter privately. "If we have done anything wrong," Morgan had said in a White House meeting with Roosevelt, "send your man to my man and they can fix it up."

The same Supreme Court that ruled against J. P. Morgan also ruled against the inhabitants of the Territory of Puerto Rico. The Court declared that although they were not aliens who could be refused admission to the United States, they were also not citizens.

In Boston, on the day two politicians went to jail for corruption (they'd taken civil service exams on behalf of applicants), voters elected them to the offices of alderman and state representative. "They did it for their friends," one voter explained.

In *McClure's Magazine*, Lincoln Steffens, the managing editor, wrote a sensational series of exposés about corruption in city government that went well beyond taking civil service exams for friends. Collected in *The Shame of Cities*, Steffens's essays described how businessmen and politicians made each other rich with taxpayer money. Two years later, Roosevelt condemned such reporting as "muckraking."

MARKETING, BUSINESS, AND MANUFACTURING

For the first time, Montgomery Ward began to distribute free catalog to its customers. Sears, Roebuck and Montgomery Ward mailed a total of 4 million free catalogs in the spring of 1904.

Chain tobacco stores began to use coupons to promote the sale of cigarettes. In New York, a woman was arrested for smoking a cigarette while riding in an open motor car on Fifth Avenue. "You can't do that on Fifth Avenue," said the policeman.

The Tropical Fruit Steamship Company, a subsidiary of United Fruit, became the first company to install radios on all its ships. Ship captains used them to learn where and when bananas could be loaded.

In Detroit, Henry Leland formed the Cadillac Motor Car Company. Also in Detroit, the George N. Pierce Company began to produce Great Arrow luxury cars. In its first year, the Pierce Company produced fifty

Great Arrows and sold them for between $3,000 and $5,000 each. In Lansing, Ramsun Olds left the Oldsmobile Company in a dispute over the size and price of the company's vehicles.

SPORTS, FOOD, BOOKS, SONGS, AND GOOD DEEDS

In baseball, Cy Young of the Boston Americans pitched the first major league no-hitter. Also, the World Series was canceled when the owner of the National League's New York Giants refused to let his team play the American League's Boston Red Sox. The Giants' owner said he'd been insulted by remarks made by the owner of the Red Sox.

In Washington, President Roosevelt popularized jujitsu by taking regular lessons in the White House from a Japanese instructor.

In St. Louis, the first Olympics ever held in the United States took place at the Louisiana Purchase Exposition. At the Fair—as the Exposition was called— three foods were sold that soon became nationally popular: the hamburger (sold by German immigrants resident in St. Louis), the ice cream cone (sold by a Syrian pastry maker to a neighboring ice cream stand that had run out of dishes), and iced tea (sold by the proprietor of an English tea stand).

Books published: Henry James's *The Golden Bowl*, Jack London's *The Sea Wolf*, and Ida Tarbell's *The History of Standard Oil*.

Popular Songs: "Frankie and Johnny" (originally "He Done Me Wrong" or "The Death of Bill Bailey"), "Give My Regards to Broadway," and "Meet Me in St. Louis, Louis."

In Pittsburgh, Andrew Carnegie gave $5 million to endow a Hero Fund to honor men and women who had risked or lost their lives rescuing others. Carnegie had been inspired by a coal mine disaster near Pittsburgh: 200 men and boys had died in an explosion and cave-in. Among them were an engineer and a miner who'd gone down the shaft to save their friends.

CITYSCAPES

In St. Louis, at the Fair, Ellsworth Statler built a 2,200-room hotel.

In Chicago, Daniel Burnham, the architect of New York's Flatiron Building, completed Orchestra Hall. Also in Chicago, Unity Temple, designed by Frank Lloyd Wright, was completed. It was the first building designed to be built entirely of poured concrete.

In New York City, the first tunnel (the Morton Street Tunnel) ever built under the Hudson River was completed. The first subway line opened. Running from the Brooklyn Bridge, north, to 145th Street, the subway carried 350,000 people on its third day of operation.

At Forty-second Street and Broadway, the *New York Times* moved into a new, twenty-five-story building. The area around it, called Longacre Square, was renamed in honor of the newspaper.

STRIKES

Twenty-five thousand textile workers in Fall River, Massachusetts, began a strike for higher wages. The strike ended six months later when mill owners accepted the workers' demands.

FOREIGN POLICY

The United States occupied the Canal Zone in Panama. Colonel George Washington Goethals of the U.S. Army Corps of Engineers oversaw the canal's construction. Surgeon General William Gorgas was sent to the Zone to direct efforts to suppress yellow fever.

DISASTERS

A huge fire in Baltimore burned for thirty hours and destroyed 2,600 buildings in an eighty-block area of the city's business district. The fire was the worst thing to happen to an American city since the Chicago Fire of 1871. Two months later, a similar fire destroyed much of Toronto, Canada.

In New York City, an excursion steamer, headed for a church picnic, carrying mostly women and children from the city's German American community, caught fire and sank in the East River. Of the 1,400 people on board, more than 1,000 drowned.

012585. MOUNT PLEASANT HOUSE, WHITE MOUNTAINS.

071251. EIGHTH GREEN, STEVENS HOUSE GOLF LINKS, LAKE PLACID, ADIRONDACK MTS. N. Y.

017113. TENNIS AT MANHANSET HOUSE, SHELTER ISLAND, N.Y.   COPYRIGHT 1904 BY DETROIT PHOTOGRAPHIC CO.

016848. ON LAKE MINNEWASKA, N.Y.

017784. LAKE FROM THE PIAZZA, FORT WILLIAM HENRY HOTEL, LAKE GEORGE, N.Y.

COPR. DETROIT PHOTOGRAPHIC CO.

SAGAMORE

017143. THE SAGAMORE DOCK, GREEN ISLAND, LAKE GEORGE, N.Y.

013530. THE "SHOO-FLY" AT MADAM BOYLE'S BAY ST. LOUIS, MISS.   DETROIT PHOTOGRAPHIC CO.

Public Power: Mills, Bridges, and Blast Furnaces

Dutiful Employees and Giant Machines

09076. TIMBERING OF A SLOPE.

01615 PLYMOUTH COAL BREAKER, PA.

1905

FOREIGN POLICY

President Roosevelt helped negotiate a peace treaty between Russia and Japan, concluding what may have been the first modern war. Hostilities ended after Japanese naval forces destroyed a Russian fleet of eight battleships, twelve cruisers, and nine destroyers in forty-five minutes, from a distance of four miles. A year later, Roosevelt was awarded the Nobel Peace Prize for his mediation efforts. Roosevelt's success as a mediator was based, in part, on a private agreement between the U.S. and Japan in which the U.S. recognized Korea as within Japan's sphere of influence in return for Japanese acknowledgment of comparable interests in the Philippines.

Following the default of the Dominican Republic on its international debts, President Roosevelt negotiated a protocol that took charge of the Republic's customs and payments while guaranteeing its territorial integrity. Roosevelt legitimized his action by declaring a corollary to the Monroe Doctrine: "In flagrant cases of wrongdoing and incompetence," the President wrote, the United States might "exercise...an international police power" in the hemisphere.

DOMESTIC EVENTS AND POLICIES

Under the leadership of Atlanta University professor W. E. B. Du Bois, twenty-nine African American intellectuals founded the Niagara Movement to abolish racism in the United States. In 1909, following race riots in Springfield, Illinois, the Niagara Movement joined with white socialists and liberals to form the National Association for the Advancement of Colored People.

In Chicago, Robert S. Abbott published the first issue of the *Chicago Defender*, the first African American newspaper of national influence. Within twelve years, the *Defender* became so widely read in the South that it inspired massive black migration to northern cities.

In Washington, the Supreme Court upheld the right of Massachusetts—and all states—to enforce compulsory vaccination laws. At the same time, the Massachusetts state legislature voted against a bill requiring patent medicines to carry labels showing their ingredients. This, in spite of an exposé in the *Ladies' Home Journal* revealing many patent medicines to be nothing but concoctions of alcohol, morphine, and cocaine. A second article, published in *Collier's*, revealed why newspapers often led the fight against such legislation: the patent medicine industry spent $40 million a year in advertising, much of it in newspapers and much of it negotiated with contracts that could be canceled in the event of hostile legislation.

Upton Sinclair's bestseller *The Jungle* made Americans even more nervous about what they ingested. With an advance of $500 from the Socialist periodical *Appeal to Reason*, Sinclair spent seven weeks with stockyard workers in Chicago. There he saw sausage made with poisoned rats and lard mixed with what was left of workers who'd fallen into the boiling vats.

In an article in the *Ladies' Home Journal*, former president Grover Cleveland wrote that "sensible and responsible women do not want to vote." The man who had begun his career as a reform mayor of Buffalo and ended it by sending federal troops to break the Pullman strike wrote, "The relative positions assigned by men and women in the working out of our civilization were assigned long ago by a higher intelligence than ours."

In Washington, President Roosevelt created the Bureau of Forestry inside the Department of Agriculture and named Gifford Pinchot to be the bureau's chief forester. Pinchot led an effort to create forest reserves and protect public lands from private developers. Pinchot lasted into the Taft administration, when he accused Taft's interior secretary of giving away Alaskan coal deposits to a syndicate. Taft fired him in 1910.

LABOR AND CLASS CONFLICT

The Supreme Court declared unconstitutional a New York State law that limited working hours (in the baking industry) to sixty hours per week.

In Chicago, members of the radical Western Federation of Miners, led by "Big Bill" Haywood, formed a new union called the International Workers of the World. One of the IWW's first actions was to condemn Samuel Gomper and his American Federation of Labor for "conniving with capitalists." Within a year, Haywood was arrested and charged with the assassination of the former governor of Idaho, Frank Steuenberg. The lawyer Clarence Darrow, who later defended a Tennessee school teacher named Scopes for teaching the theories of Charles Darwin, defended Haywood and, in 1907, won his acquittal.

TECHNOLOGY AND MANUFACTURING

In Dayton, the Wright Brothers demonstrated their aircraft to the public by flying a twenty-four-mile circle in thirty-eight minutes.

The Stanley Steamer automobile set a speed record of 127 miles an hour. Unfortunately, the Steamer required a thirty-minute warm-up and fresh water every twenty miles.

The Long Island Railroad became the first American railroad to replace its coal-fired steam locomotives with engines powered by electricity from a low-voltage third rail.

The Chicago and Northwestern Railroad installed electric lights, for the first time, on a passenger train running from Chicago to California.

The Pennsylvania Railroad and the New York Central Railroad inaugurated eighteen-hour train service between New York City and Chicago. The New York Central called its train the "Twentieth Century Limited."

American automobile manufacturers produced 25,000 cars in 1905. Six years earlier, they'd made only 2,500.

MARKETING

The Murad Cigarette Company was the first tobacco company to use the testimonials of famous entertainers to sell cigarettes.

MOVIES, NEWS, ART, BOOKS, AND SPORTS

The first storefront movie theater, called a nickelodeon, opened in Pittsburgh. Within three years, there were 10,000 of them in cities and towns all across the United States

In New York, *Variety* began publication. Also in New York, the photographer Alfred Stieglitz opened Gallery 291 on Fifth Avenue.

Books published: Edith Wharton's *The House of Mirth*, and Thomas Dixon's novel about the Ku Klux Klan, *The Clansman*. D. W. Griffith based his 1915 film *Birth of a Nation* on Dixon's novel.

The Detroit Tigers signed Ty Cobb as an outfielder.

In the World Series, the New York Giants' Christy Mathewson pitched three shutouts against the Philadelphia Athletics.

CITYSCAPES

Wildcat prospectors struck a huge pool of oil at Red Fort, in Indian Territory, across the Arkansas River from what had been a trading post called Tulsey Town. Their discovery turned Tulsey into Tulsa, and Tulsa into the "Oil Capital of the World."

In New York City, the population density of some of its slums was 1,000 persons per acre. Not even sections of Bombay matched that density.

Also in New York: The highest price ever paid for a piece of real estate was paid for a 1,250-square-foot lot at No. 1 Wall Street. The lot sold for $700,000 (in 1905 dollars).

DISASTERS

One thousand people died of yellow fever in New Orleans. An antimosquito campaign by the U.S. Public Health Service ended the epidemic. It would be the last yellow fever epidemic in the United States.

UNLOADING ORE AT CONNEAUT, OHIO.
BROWN CONVEYING HOISTS.

2301 BROWN ELECTRIC HOIST UNLOADING ORE BUFFALO, N.Y.

6980. DUMPING SLAG.   BESS. STEEL WORKS.   W.H. JACKSON PHOTO & PUB. CO.

CITYSCAPES AND DISASTERS

An earthquake, followed by three days of fire, destroyed much of San Francisco. Efforts by the military to create fire-breaks and collapse dangerous buildings using explosives only spread the flames. At least 700 people died; 250,000 were made homeless; approximately 25,000 buildings were destroyed. Although many more people died in Galveston in 1900, the scale of the destruction far exceeded what had happened to Baltimore and Toronto in 1904 or to Jacksonville in 1901.

Damage was estimated at $400 million (in 1906 dollars). Reconstruction loans, made by banker Amadeo Giannini in gold coins rescued from his vault, led to other loans that turned his little Bank of Italy into what would become the largest private banking system in the world, the Bank of America.

Six months after the earthquake, the San Francisco Board of Education ordered the segregation of all Oriental children in city schools. The order was rescinded after protests by the Japanese ambassador.

HOMICIDES

In New York, architect Stanford White was shot and killed by Pittsburgh millionaire Harry K. Thaw during a musical revue in a restaurant on the roof of Madison Square Garden—a building White had designed in 1890. Thaw's lawyers claimed his client had been incapacitated by "a brainstorm" of jealousy when he learned that his wife, a former chorus girl named Evelyn Nesbit, had once been White's mistress. After a hung jury, Thaw was acquitted because of insanity. He was committed to a mental hospital, but escaped, was captured, and committed again.

In upstate New York, Chester Gillet, a foreman in a shirtwaist factory owned by his uncle, murdered Grace Brown, one of his employees and the daughter of a local farmer. Gillet rowed Brown out into the middle of a lake and murdered her after she told him she was pregnant. Gillet said he did it because he wanted to marry a society girl he'd met.

Both homicides made headlines in the United States and in Europe. Gillet's murder of Grace Brown became the basis of Theodore Dreiser's novel *An American Tragedy*.

DOMESTIC EVENTS AND POLICIES

A race riot occurred in Brownsville, Texas, following a series of incidents in which several African American soldiers from a segregated infantry battalion stationed nearby came to town and "shot it up." Whether this was a reprisal or not was never learned. After reports of a rape and a murder, townspeople took revenge. What actually happened and in what order was never determined. In the end, President Roosevelt ordered the dishonorable discharge of three companies of troops.

In Washington, Congress granted U.S. citizenship to the Five Civilized Tribes—the Cherokee, Chicksaw, Chocktaw, Creek, and Seminoles—all of whom had been forced to resettle, seventy-five years earlier, in Indian Territory in Oklahoma. A year later, Congress granted statehood to Oklahoma and opened the territory to white settlement.

In New York City, a gathering of mostly German Jews, alarmed by the increase in anti-Semitism following recent Jewish immigration from Poland and Russia, formed the American Jewish Committee to protect the rights of Jews in the United States and abroad.

In Washington, Congress passed a series of unprecedented regulatory acts. The first, an act "for the preservation of American antiquities," gave the president the power to set aside historic landmarks and phenomena of nature as "national monuments." President Roosevelt promptly designated Devil's Tower in Wyoming as the country's first National Monument.

The second regulatory bill passed by Congress was the Railroad Rate Act. The bill—supplementing the Interstate Commerce Act of 1887—gave the federal government the authority to set rates for the interstate shipment of products and raw materials.

The final act, passed in large part in response to such exposés as Upton Sinclair's *The Jungle* and Samuel Adams's *The Great American Fraud* (a collection of articles about patent medicines, first published in *Collier's*), was the Pure Food and Drug Act. During the debate on the bill, one of its sponsors in the House read, into the record, a short list of items added to coffee: "Colored with: Sheele's green, iron oxide, yellow ocher, chrome yellow, burnt umber, Venetian red, turmeric, Prussian blue, indigo.

Adulterated with: roasted peas, beans, wheat, rye, oats, chicory, brown bread, charcoal, red slate, bark, date stones." The Senate passed the bill and sent it to the president, following pressure from the American Medical Association.

President Roosevelt began to distance himself from the reformers who wrote and edited such magazines as *McClure's* and *Collier's.* "The men with the muckrakes," Roosevelt said, alluding to a passage in Bunyon's *Pilgrim Progress,* "are often indispensable to the well-being of society, but only when they know when to stop raking the muck and...look...upward...to the crown of worthy endeavor."

TRUSTS, AGRIBUSINESS, AND CLASS CONFLICT

U.S. Steel broke ground for a new plant on the southern shore of Lake Michigan. The company town that grew up around it was named after the corporation's chairman, Elbert Gary.

J. P. Morgan and steel mill owner John "Bet a Million" Gates bought the Tennessee Coal and Iron Company.

E. I. Du Pont de Nemours took over the Powder Trust, a thirty-four-year-old association of gunpowder manufacturers. By doing so, Du Pont monopolized the production of gunpowder and five other kinds of explosives in the United States.

Standard Oil Director E. T. Bedford formed the Corn Products Refining Company. The company controlled 90 percent of all corn refining in the United States. Its Karo Syrup became nearly the only such product available.

In Texas, the King Ranch grew to cover 1 million acres, with 75,000 head of cattle and 10,000 horses.

In California, 17 million acres of farmland in the Sacramento Valley came to be owned by 100 men.

The anarchist Alexander Berkman was released from prison. He had been sent to jail after he'd tried—and failed—to kill Henry Clay Frick, the chairman of Carnegie Steel, during the Homestead Strike of 1892. Once released, Berkman rejoined his lover, Emma Goldman, and with her, founded the radical journal *Mother Earth.* In 1917, the federal government ordered it closed. In 1919,

following a postwar depression and strikes involving 4 million U.S. workers, Goldman, Berkman, and 500 other anarchists, communists, and subversives were deported. Their deportation followed FBI raids ordered by U.S. Attorney General Palmer. The strikes, followed by the raids, came to be known as the "Red Scare."

MANUFACTURING AND MARKETING

In Detroit, W. C. Durant's Buick Company produced 2,295 cars. Just two years earlier, the company had made only 28.

In Allentown, John, William, and August Mack built the first Mack truck.

In Hartford, Connecticut, Alfred Fuller, who made and then sold his own brushes, door to door, founded the Fuller Brush Company.

In Battle Creek, Michigan, W. K. and J. H. Kellogg started the Battle Creek Toasted Corn Flake Company. Two-thirds of the company's budget went to advertising.

Annual sales of Jell-O reached $1 million.

In Wilkes-Barre, Pennsylvania, Amedeo Obici founded Planters Nut and Chocolate Company. Obici had begun with a peanut stand. Within six years, Planters built its own shelling plant and began to buy peanuts directly from southern growers.

TECHNOLOGY

The first radio broadcast of voice and music was transmitted from Brandt Rock, Massachusetts, by Reginald Fressenden.

Lee De Forest added a third electrode to an already existing two-electrode vacuum tube. The result greatly enhanced radio reception.

MUSICALS, SONGS, AND MARRIAGE

In New York, George M. Cohan produced *Forty-five Minutes from Broadway* and *George Washington, Jr.*

Popular songs: "Anchors Aweigh" and "You're a Grand Old Flag."

Alice Lee Roosevelt, the beautiful and headstrong daughter of President Roosevelt, married Congressman Nicholas Longworth in the White House.

09759 STUYVESANT ELEVATORS, R.R. TERMINALS, NEW ORLEANS.

DETROIT PHOTOGRAPHIC CO.

012560 WATER TOWER AND SHOPS ENTRANCE PULLMAN ILLS.

Freighters and Destroyers

Shipyards, Sailors, and a Two Ocean Navy

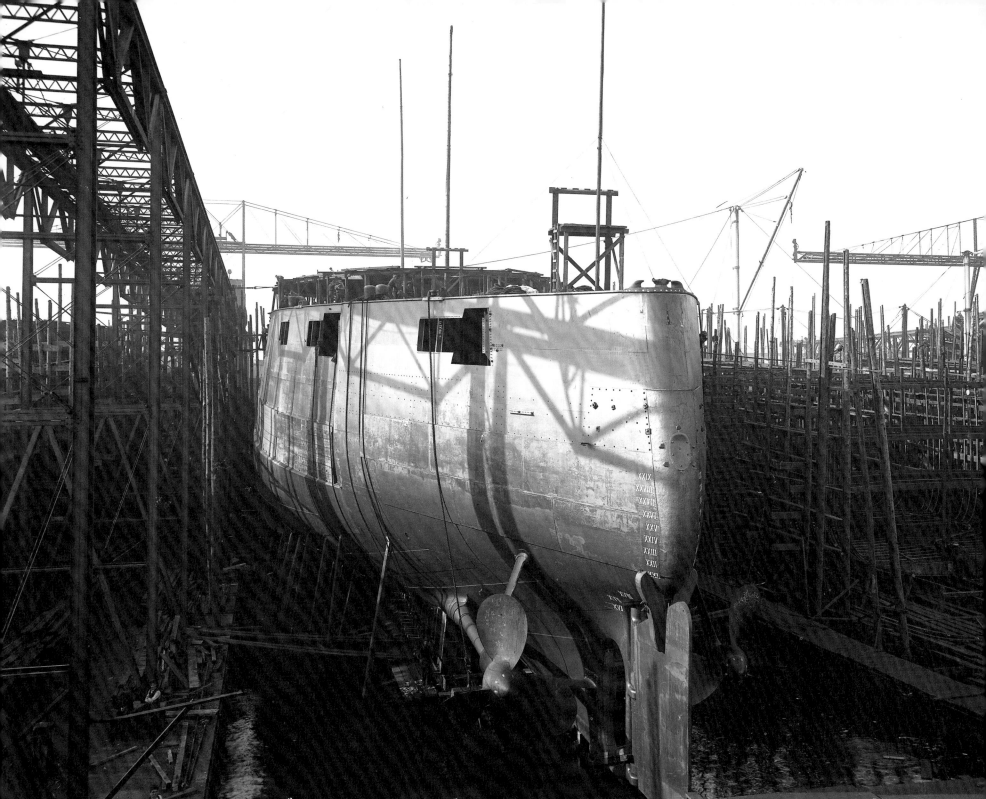

RUSSIAN WAR SHIP "RETVIZAN," DAY BEFORE LAUNCHING,   DETROIT PHOTOGRAPHIC CO.

022285. LAUNCH OF S.S. W.E. FITZGERALD.

DETROIT OF DETROIT

022164. STR. HOOVER AND MASON, AFTER THE LAUNCH.

DETROIT PUBLISHING CO.

1907

A FINANCIAL PANIC

A shortage of cash, credit, and specie—a liquidity crisis—created a financial panic that, for a time, threatened a collapse of the country's banks—and its economy. The panic began with a sudden collapse of prices on the New York Stock Exchange. Depositors rushed to withdraw cash from accounts at New York's Knickerbocker Trust Company. When the trust company (which had less stringent cash reserve requirements than a "national" bank) couldn't satisfy demand, it closed its doors. Bank runs followed in Pittsburgh and Providence and, again in New York, against the Trust Company of America.

The crisis in the money supply was later explained as the result of capital drains caused by the Russo-Japanese War; a succession of financial panics in Japan, Egypt, and Chile; the San Francisco earthquake; and several large-scale domestic railway-construction projects. Whatever the causes, the federal government turned to J. P. Morgan to function as its central banker.

Morgan did everything from securing bridge loans of tens of millions of dollars from several banks and financiers, to pledging $30 million of his own (at 6 percent interest) to the City of New York to prevent default on its short-term bonds, to literally locking-up (in his library, overnight) the presidents of several New York trust companies, until they signed a loan to bailout the Trust Company of America. Morgan even imported $10 million in gold from the Bank of England, ordering it transported on board the *Lusitania*, the fastest ship to cross the Atlantic. The federal Government did its part by issuing $150 million in assorted certificates and bonds at low interest rates and allowing banks to issue currency on the bonds as collateral.

Besides earning the respect and prestige he deserved for what he did, Morgan earned something else: in the midst of the crisis, he was able to convince President Roosevelt to approve his acquisition (with mill owner and speculator John W. Gates) of the Tennessee Coal and Iron Company—even though that acquisition violated the Sherman Anti-Trust Act.

DOMESTIC POLICY

In federal district court in Illinois, Judge Kenesaw Mountain Landis fined Standard Oil of Indiana (a subsidiary of J. D. Rockefeller's Standard Oil of New Jersey) $29 million for having received secret, illegal rebates for rail shipments of crude oil. Although Landis's decision was overturned on appeal, his stand against corruption led to his appointment in 1919 as baseball commissioner after the World Series Black Sox scandals.

In Washington, President Roosevelt signed an immigration act that gave him the right to prevent Japanese laborers, emigrating from Canada, Mexico, or Hawaii from entering the continental United States. Having signed the bill, the president ordered the exclusions.

FOREIGN POLICY

President Roosevelt ordered a squadron of sixteen U.S. battleships, known as the Great White Fleet, to "show the flag" around the world. Roosevelt's intent was to advertise the United States as a global power. In particular, he meant to impress the Japanese with this country's "big stick."

MANUFACTURING

American automobile manufacturers produced 43,000 vehicles, nearly double the number of the year before.

Vincent Bendix founded the Bendix Company to produce automobile starter drives. Within five years, his "self-starters" would replace hand cranks in automobiles.

Bethlehem Steel began to produce wide-flanged beams that were lighter and cheaper but just as strong as conventional steel girders.

In Iowa, a farm equipment company built and sold the first Maytag washing machine. The company's owner, Frederick Maytag, devised the machine as a way to keep the company working during seasonal lulls in the farm equipment business.

MARKETING

In Dallas, A. L. Neiman, his wife, Carrie, and his brother-in-law, Herbert Marcus, opened a department store with money from the sale of their Atlanta advertising agency to the Coca-Cola Company. Within a month, they had sold nearly every evening gown, fur coat, tailored suit, dress, and hat in the store. Coca-Cola had offered them company stock and a franchise for the whole state of Missouri, but they'd taken the money and moved to a town that had one saloon for every 400 inhabitants.

CITYSCAPES

The Plaza Hotel opened in New York. Designed by Henry J. Hardenbergh (who also designed the Waldorf, the Willard, and the Astor hotels), the Plaza's 1,000-room French Renaissance Beaux-Arts style exemplified the decade's ambitions to grand luxury.

Union Station opened in Washington. Daniel Burnham, the architect of New York's Flatiron Building, derived his design for the station from the Baths of Diocletian and the Arch of Constantine.

In San Francisco, the mayor of the city urged that a river in Yosemite be damned to provide the city with a water source more reliable than those that had failed during the earthquake and fire. John Muir, the naturalist, who had spent six years studying the forests and geology of Yosemite, opposed the plan. Muir was supported by President Roosevelt's chief forester, Gifford Pinchot, who— for the first time—used the word "conservation" to press his argument.

SEX, MOVIES, SPORTS, CARTOONS, AND A MEMOIR

The first Ziegfeld Follies, featuring "the most beautiful girls in the world," opened on Broadway.

Elinor Glyn's *Three Weeks*, a novel about an illicit affair, was banned in Boston. Within a month, it sold 50,000 copies.

In Cleveland, the first color motion picture with sound was shown. Scenes from an opera, a bullfight, and a political speech were shown with sound effects.

Rube Goldberg began to draw cartoons of elaborate and foolish machines for the *New York Evening Journal*.

In the World Series, the Chicago Cubs beat the Detroit Tigers with flawless double plays executed by shortstop Joe Tinker, second baseman Johnny Evers, and first baseman Frank Chance. "Tinker to Evers to Chance" came to mean any flawlessly executed act.

Henry Adams privately published his rueful memoir *The Education of Henry Adams*.

DISASTERS

One of the worst mine disasters in United States history killed 361 men and boys in Monongah, West Virginia. Twelve years later, a mine explosion in Jacobs Creek, Pennsylvania, killed 239 men.

020438 - U.S.S. IOWA. 12 INCH AND 8 INCH GUN TURRETS.   DETROIT PHOTOGRAPHIC CO.

U.S.S. MASSACHUSETTS, INTERIOR OF TURRET.   DETROIT PHOTOGRAPHIC CO.

Pickaninnies and Prisoners

DOMESTIC POLITICS AND POLICIES

President Roosevelt declined to run for another term even though he would have been easily reelected. Instead he chose his own successor: William Howard Taft. Taft had begun as a lawyer, then a state supreme court judge in Cincinnati. William McKinley had appointed him civil governor of the Philippines; Roosevelt made him Secretary of War.

Taft was an amiable mediocrity who had risen to power because of the wealth and influence of his family. Not once had he run for office. In New York City, when asked at the end of a speech meant to launch his campaign, "What is a man to do if out of work and starving?" Taft had answered, "God knows, I don't." Roosevelt's closest advisers were alarmed, but Roosevelt stood by his protégé and friend.

The result was a boring campaign against a broken-down William Jennings Bryan, nominated for a third time by the Democrats. The Socialist Party nominated Eugene V. Debs; the Socialist Labor Party nominated Martin Preston even though Preston was in the Nevada Penitentiary, convicted of murder. During the campaign, Taft played more golf than he gave speeches. The outcome of the election was 7.6 million votes for Taft, 6.4 for Bryan. Third parties, including the Prohibitionist Party, won 5 percent of the vote. As soon as Taft was inaugurated, Roosevelt left for Africa to go big game hunting with his son, under the auspices of the Smithsonian.

In Washington, the Supreme Court handed down three major decisions against organized labor: it confirmed prison sentences against three American Federation of Labor officers—including the AFL's president, Samuel Gompers —for violating an injunction against a boycott of a stove company; it upheld the firing of a railroad employee for belonging to a union, ruling that a recent law that prohibited discrimination against union labor in interstate commerce violated the Fifth Amendment; and, in a famous case—the Danbury Hatters case—the Court ruled that the Sherman Anti-Trust Act applied to unions as well as corporations and that a nationwide boycott against a Connecticut hatmaker was a conspiracy in restraint of trade.

ALSO IN WASHINGTON

The Federal Bureau of Investigation was formed inside the Justice Department. One of the bureau's few, early responsibilities was to investigate the interstate transport of stolen automobiles. Not until 1919, after raids led by Attorney General Palmer against what Palmer claimed was a national communist conspiracy of immigrants, did the bureau become politically powerful and prominent.

Before leaving office, President Roosevelt declared Arizona's Grand Canyon and a 500-acre tract of first growth redwoods and sequoias in California—known as Muir Woods—to be National Monuments. He also convened a Conservation Conference at the White House to which he invited the governors of forty-four states and territories.

BUSINESS AND MARKETING

J. C. Penney bought out his partner and began a chain of department stores, headquartered in Salt Lake City. By 1911, Penney had 22 stores; by 1913, he had 48. By 1916, he had 127 stores and moved his headquarters to New York.

CITYSCAPES

Unemployment, caused by the financial panic of 1907, continued to spread. In New York City, the Bowery Mission reported it was feeding 2,000 more men than before. Unemployed workers filled newspapers with personal ads, declaring themselves willing to work for food.

Race riots in Springfield, Illinois, were reported on by New York journalist William Walling. A year later, the first meeting of the National Association for the Advancement of Colored People was held in Walling's Greenwich Village apartment. Of the more than fifty prominent people who founded the NAACP, only six of them, including its president, W. E. B. Du Bois, were African American.

In New York, the forty-seven-story Singer Building, built as the headquarters of the Singer Sewing Machine Company, became the tallest building in the world. A year later, the fifty-story Metropolitan Life Tower surpassed it. Met Life held the record until 1913 when the sixty-story Woolworth Building rose above it.

The same year the Woolworth Building was finished, three other New York landmarks were completed: Grand Central Terminal at Forty-second Street, the Equitable Building on lower Broadway, and the General Post Office Building on Eighth Avenue, across from Pennsylvania Station. Above the corinthian columns of the post office, the architectural firm of McKim, Mead, and White inscribed words written by the historian Heroditus to describe the messengers of Xerxes, the King of Persia: "Neither snow, nor rain, nor heat, nor gloom of night stays these couriers from the swift completion of their appointed rounds."

Underground in New York, two new subway tunnels opened: a tunnel under the Hudson to Hoboken, and a tunnel under the East River, from Bowling Green to Brooklyn.

Also in New York: Eight painters known as the Ashcan school, presented the first exhibition of their work in a group show at the McBeth Gallery. Their style, influenced by Thomas Eakins, was realist and representational. They painted urban scenes and urban subjects: backyards, crowded streets, and solitary watchers.

In Worcester, Massachusetts, voters banned the sale and consumption of alcohol. Worcester became the largest city in the United States to order prohibition.

In Philadelphia, prohibitionist and suffragette Anna May Jarris celebrated the first Mother's Day.

Elsewhere: At nickelodeons in cities across the country, an estimated 200,000 customers per day—most of them working class, many of them immigrants—paid to see six ten-minute films at a time. A typical show included an adventure, a comedy, a chase film, a melodrama, and a documentary. The first film censorship occurred in New York City when the mayor forced theater owners to sign a pledge not to show immoral films and not to show movies on Sundays.

RESEARCH, TECHNOLOGY, AND MANUFACTURING

After nine years of research, Carl Wheaton of Newtonville, Massachusetts, announced he had developed a poison gas that could be used as a weapon against infantry. Wheaton offered his formula to the U.S. Army.

Wilbur Wright built his first airplane for the War Department. During a test flight, it crashed, killing an army Signal Corps lieutenant who'd sat next to Wright as his passenger. A year later, a second plane completed tests requiring it to carry two men for sixty minutes, at forty miles an hour.

In Houston, Howard R. Hughes founded the Hughes Tool Company. Hughes's steel-toothed, rock-drilling bits, using rolling-cone cutters, revolutionized oil drilling.

In Detroit, Henry Ford introduced his wood-bodied, steel-framed Model T. Its $850 price was $100 more than a year's minimum wage.

Harvey S. Firestone sold Ford 2,000 sets of tires for his new Model Ts. Firestone's sale began a business relationship that lasted more than thirty years.

Frank Stranahan and his brother, Robert, began the Champion Spark Plug Company in a garage in Boston. Two years later, they moved their operations to Toledo and sold their first order of spark plugs to Henry Ford. Champion would supply Ford with spark plugs for the next fifty years.

In Detroit, W. C. Durant, the president of Buick Motor Car Company, formed General Motors. Within a year, GM would absorb the Buick, Olds, Cadillac, and Oakland motor car companies. Henry Ford offered to sell his company to Durant for $8 million in cash, but Durant's bankers advised him that Ford's company wasn't worth the price.

That year, a total of twenty-four automobile manufacturing companies made 63,500 cars. There were 200,000 cars on the road. In 1900, there had been 8,000.

Vistas, Wild and Domestic, Scenic and Unsettled

Massive Forms and Enormous Spaces

072019, LOOKING SOUTH FROM MT. TOM, MASS.

1909

FOREIGN POLICY

In a so-called gentleman's agreement, the government of Japan agreed not to issue any more passports to workers seeking to immigrate to the United States.

A year later, the military theorist Homer Lea predicted in his book, *The Valor of Ignorance*, that war between the United States and Japan was inevitable. Lea predicted that the Japanese would strike first—against the Philippines, then move on to Hawaii, Alaska, and finally, California. Lea had graduated from Stanford Law School, then traveled to China, and became a close adviser to the Chinese revolutionary, Sun Yat-sen.

CARTOONS, SONGS, SPORTS, AND THE NEWS

"Mutt and Jeff," drawn by Bud Fisher, appeared in the *San Francisco Examiner*. "Mutt and Jeff" was the first cartoon to appear daily with the same characters.

Popular songs: "Take Me Out to the Ball Game," "She Sells Sea Shells," and

African American Jack Johnson won the world heavyweight boxing championship by beating Tommy Burns in Sydney, Australia. Police stopped the bout after fourteen rounds.

The University of Missouri opened the first professional School of Journalism in the United States.

DISASTERS

In Cleveland, a fire in a public school killed 176 children and their teachers.

In Chelsea, near Boston, a fire on Palm Sunday burned down a third of the town.

An explosion and a cave-in at a Union Pacific Coal Company mine in Hanna, Wyoming, killed sixty miners.

One hundred more miners died in a cave-in at the Marianna Mine in Monongahela, Pennsylvania.

RESEARCH AND EXPLORATION

Thomas Hunt Morgan, a professor of experimental zoology at Columbia University, conducted extensive breeding experiments with the fruit fly, *Drosophila melanogaster*. The result was the chromosome theory of heredity— an understanding that individual units of heredity, known as genes, were arranged in a line of chromosomes in the nucleus of each cell. Morgan went on to theorize, in monographs written over the next sixteen years, that each gene was responsible for the manufacture of a particular protein that, itself, was involved in the development of a particular trait.

U.S. Navy engineer Robert E. Perry, accompanied by Matt Henson, an African American, and four Eskimos, claimed, in a telegram to the New York Times, to have reached latitude 90 degrees north. "I have the Pole....," Perry cabled. It had taken him six expeditions, over the course of twenty years, to reach it. The National Geographic Society supported Perry's claim and, in 1911, he was made a rear admiral.

DOMESTIC POLICY

The Senate passed the Sixteenth Amendment to the Constitution and sent it on to the states for ratification. The Amendment authorized Congress to impose an income tax. The first income tax (a graduated tax on incomes above $3,000) was levied in 1913.

Congress passed a copyright law. The law would remain unchanged for the next sixty-eight years.

Congress banned the import of opium for anything but medical purposes.

1909

FOREIGN POLICY

Two U.S. warships were sent to Nicaragua after 500 rebels, including two Americans, were executed by the country's dictator, José Zelaya. More warships and the threat of a U.S. invasion persuaded Zelaya to "retire" a week before Christmas.

STRIKES

Twenty thousand garment workers, members of the Ladies Waist Makers Union, a local of the International Ladies Garment Workers, began a three-month strike. The strikers won most of their demands, but working conditions remained appalling. Two years later, a fire in a sweatshop—the Triangle Shirtwaist Factory—killed 146 women.

MARKETING

The Hawaiian Pineapple Growers Association, led by James Dole, began the first ad campaign undertaken by a growers' association. Dole's marketing campaign increased the sale of canned pineapples in cities along the East Coast.

PUBLISHING

In New York City, the *Amsterdam News* began publication. It became the largest, nonreligious, African American weekly in the United States.

CITYSCAPES

In New York City, two new bridges—the Manhattan and the Queensboro—opened within ten months of each other.

In Chicago, Frank Lloyd Wright completed the Robie House. It was the first house to be built on a slab foundation, to incorporate automobile garages in its structure, and to use indirect electric lighting and rheostats.

In Washington, the first International Conference on City Planning convened. In his "Plan for Chicago of 1909," the architect Daniel Burnham wrote, "Make no little plans... [Little plans] have no magic to stir men's blood."

SONGS AND ANIMATION

Popular songs: "On Wisconsin" and "By the Light of the Silvery Moon."

Windsor McCay, cartoonist for the New York American, used 10,000 drawings to animate the film *Gertie the Dinosaur.*

DISASTERS

An explosion at the St. Paul Mine in Cherry, Illinois, killed 259 men and boys.

INTERIOR OF THE GARDEN.

04837 RACINE, WIS. CEDAR BEND. ROOT RIVER.
COPYRIGHT 1898 DETROIT PHOTOGRAPHIC CO.

Natives in Costume

Real Men

Co

07177. MINERS AT HOME

MAIN ST. TELLURIDE.

Dreams at the Edge of an Ocean

1910

SOME FACTS AT THE END OF THE DECADE

The United States Census Bureau recorded a population of 92 million people. Half of them lived in towns of 2,500 or more. The center of population settlement was Bloomington, Indiana.

Eighty percent of African Americans still lived in the eleven southern states.

Less than half the United States population over twenty-five years of age had finished grade school. Only 4 percent of the population had attended college.

The average wage was less than $15 per week. Most people worked from fifty-four to sixty hours per week.

The period 1906–1910 was the deadliest time in U.S. history to be a miner. Eighty-four explosions and cave-ins killed a total of 2,494 people.

By 1910, eight states had banned the sale and consumption of alcohol: Maine, North Carolina, Tennessee, Georgia, Mississippi, Oklahoma, Kansas, and North Dakota.

DOMESTIC POLICIES AND EVENTS

Congress extended the Interstate Commerce Commission's regulatory authority to include telegraph, telephone, and cable companies.

Congress passed the Mann Act, known as the "White Slave Act," to prohibit the interstate or international transport of women for immoral purposes.

A constitutional amendment in the state of Washington granted women the right to vote. A year later, a constitutional amendment in California granted women the right to vote in that state.

In Norfolk, Virginia, a bank founded by attorney Arthur Morris made personal loans for the first time. "Morris' Plan" loans to individuals required local employment, two cosigners, and monthly installment payments at 11.6 percent interest for one year. Until Morris' bank began making such loans, individual borrowers would have to ask family or friends, or go to pawnshops or loan sharks. Within ten years, Morris Plan banks were making loans in thirty-seven states. Life on the installment plan had begun.

In Chicago, the Boy Scouts of America was founded by William Boyce, a publisher who'd been inspired by Sir Robert Baden-Powell's English Boy Scouts. Two other organizations—the Sons of Daniel Boone and the Woodcraft Indians—had preceded the Boy Scouts in the United States.

In New York City, the Camp Fire Girls was founded by Dr. Luther Gulick. Gulick had been the director of physical education, first for the YMCA, then for the New York Public Schools. Twenty years earlier, Gulick and James Naismith had invented the game of basketball in Springfield, Massachusetts.

On Independence Day, in Reno, Nevada, African American boxer Jack Johnson knocked out undefeated heavyweight champion Jim Jeffries in fifteen rounds. Jeffries had come out of a five-year retirement to fight Johnson. The press referred to Jeffries as "the great white hope." After Johnson's victory, white mobs attacked African Americans in Boston, New York, Norfolk, Cincinnati, and Houston. Three African Americans were killed by a mob in Uvalda, Georgia.

STRIKES AND A BOMBING

In New York City, members of the International Ladies Garment Workers won a nine-week strike against cloak makers.

In Los Angeles, a bomb planted by James McNamara and his brother, John, killed twenty people at the *Los Angeles Times*. The McNamaras had planted the bomb in revenge for the *Times's* opposition to organized labor. Clarence Darrow served as their lawyer, but they confessed a year later.

MANUFACTURING, TECHNOLOGY, AND RESEARCH

Frederick W. Taylor's time-and-motion studies convinced more and more factory owners to use efficiency experts to study and reform the work patterns of their employees. Such Taylor essays as "Shop Management" and "The Piece Rate System" persuaded manufacturers that they could "scientifically manage" their workers and machines.

The aviator Glen Curtiss, who had begun as a bicycle mechanic and motorcycle racer, set a new air speed record by flying from Albany to New York City in two and a half hours. A year later, Curtiss built the first successful sea plane and, a year after that, the first flying boat.

John Bray, a cartoonist for the *Brooklyn Eagle*, invented the "cel" cartoon animation, using celluloid transparencies, in layers, to create and vary each frame of an animated cartoon.

BUSINESS

Hallmark Inc. began as a wholesale card jobbing company in Kansas City.

Minnesota Mining and Manufacturing Company(3M) began in St. Paul as a manufacturer of sandpaper.

CITYSCAPES

In New York City, Pennsylvania Station opened for commuter and long-distance rail traffic. The station occupied two square blocks between Seventh and Eighth Avenues, from Thirty-first to Thirty-third Streets. It had 150-foot ceilings and eighty-four Doric columns, thirty-five feet high. The architectural firm of McKim, Mead, and White used the Baths of Caracalla in Rome as their model.

MOVIES, BOOKS, AND RELIGION

The San Francisco Board of Censors declared 32 films to be "unfit for public exhibition." Titles included *Saved by a Sailor, In Hot Pursuit, The Black Viper,* and *Maggie, the Dock Rat.*

Books published: Jane Addams's *Twenty Years at Hull House* and Eugene V. Debs's *The Growth of Socialism.* William Eliot, former president of Harvard, began publication of the fifty-volume Harvard Classics.

Also published: *The Fundamentals: A Testimony of Truth,* a summary of Christian Fundamentalist belief. These beliefs included the accuracy of the Scriptures and Virgin birth, the physical resurrection of Christ, vicarious atonement, and the physical Second Coming of Christ.

THE END OF THE WORLD

The return of Halley's Comet convinced thousands of people that the end of the world was at hand. On the day the earth crossed the comet's tail, miners refused to go below ground, while others hid in caves and cyclone cellars. Many people took comet pills to protect them from the comet's effects. In Milwaukee, two men committed suicide to avoid suffering. Mark Twain, who said he'd come in with Halley's Comet and expected to go out with it, died within a month of the comet's passing.

DREAMLAND

THE ENTERPRISE AND THE UNDERTAKING

IN 1975, A POSTCARD COLLECTOR published a guide to the Detroit Publishing Company's output; the guide listed sixty-nine images that had people or things added or subtracted from them—vanishing skyscrapers, disappearing telephone and telegraph poles, lengthened skirts, added children, more ships, more trolleys. In the photographs you've just seen, the little girl strolling down the path from Grant's Tomb, and the giant engine cylinder, floating, suspended, with a young man in it—both owe their existence to a retoucher. The very last image in the book—the picture of a man rowing down a canal in Venice, California—was the bottom half of a composite whose sky of clouds had its own negative. Scattered here and there throughout the 46,000 images that constitute the "Detroit Collection," any researcher with enough patience can find negatives that have been altered, but the alterations are so obvious (the contours of the horizon line of an ocean vista, traced with an opaquing brush to make it even more stark than it was; an automobile, excerpted from its surroundings, like the giant engine cylinder, floating in the center of a negative marked "Taken for Combination Purposes") and the instances so few, that, like the pea felt by the princess beneath her pile of mattresses, the alterations are noticeable mainly because of their rarity.

What can't be seen, though, what hides in plain sight, is much more interesting:

By the time William Livingstone died in 1924 and Detroit Publishing tumbled into receivership, it had acquired and made into postcards the work of as many as twenty-four photographers—young "camera operators" it sent out on assignment, or self-employed professionals who sold whole sets of negatives and what copyrights they owned for cash. The Company had started with a core of negatives—pictures of Great Lakes ships and shipyards, acquired by William Livingstone, whose father actually owned the things themselves: a fleet of freighters, a big Detroit bank, an important newspaper. To this was added the negatives the photographer Edwin Husher had made during his years in California. And to all these, the Company added the treasure of 10,000 western views William Henry Jackson brought with him after his own Company had crashed with the rest of the Denver economy during the depression of 1893—images Jackson had made over a period of thirty years, working for himself, the U.S. Geological Survey, and railroads like the Denver Pacific and the Denver and Rio Grande. Just as Detroit Publishing would hire camera operators and buy the work of others, so the W. H. Jackson Photographic and Printing Company had employed as many as fifty photographers in the fifteen years Jackson ran his own business.

Jackson may have presided over the small business equivalent of an atelier in Denver, but the Detroit Company was a publisher, not a museum or an art gallery. The craftsmen who worked for it; the artisans who refinished and inked the lithostones;

the flatbed press operators who rolled the card stock across them; the salesmen who hustled order after order, box after box of cards to hotel chains, railroads, and tour operators; the clerks who greeted well-to-do customers as they walked into the Company's showrooms in New York, London, and Zurich—all these people and the men who made the pictures produced a product that customers bought the way people now, standing at the newsstand in Grand Central during rush hour, might buy copies of *Time* or *Wired* or *Elle*.

In the 1950s, when Time-Life existed and Henry Luce still ruled it, cynics wrote about "Timespeak" as if it were not just a prose style but a philosophy. Detroit Publishing had the equivalent—not a speak" but a worldview. It was Edwin Husher who had told William Livingstone about the Swiss Photochrom process, and it was Husher who had let Livingstone know that William Henry Jackson, the famous photographer, was available for the right price. But as canny and acquisitive as both Husher and Livingstone were, there's no evidence that either of them had anything approaching an editorial vision.

Between 1898, when Jackson joined the Company, and 1903, when Husher moved back to California and Jackson took the title of plant manager, Jackson had two responsibilities: one was to travel and make pictures of his own; the other was to meet local photographers during his travels, look at their work, and buy their negatives. As a photographer, working for the company, Jackson was on the road for five months in 1899, taking pictures from Boston to San Diego. In 1901, he made more than 200 photographs during a month-and-a-half trip to California. (In this book, Jackson is believed to have taken the following photos: Grant's Tomb, Riverside Park, 1901; Eureka, Colorado, 1900; Washington Bridge and Speedway, Harlem River, 1901; Tampa Bay Hotel, Tampa, Florida, 1902; Hotel Chamberlain, Hampton Roads, Virginia, 1902; Atrium, West Baden Springs Hotel, West Baden, Indiana; Polishing Department, National Cash Register Company, Dayton, Ohio, 1902; "Waiting for the Sunday Boat," 1902; Silverton, Colorado, 1901; "Cowboys," no date or place.) More and more often though, when Jackson traveled, he directed crews of other photographers, while he looked, chose, and acquired the work of independents. By 1924, the Company had added 16,000 negatives to its holdings. It was Jackson who determined those acquisitions. Customers saw the world through the Company's eyes because they believed the Company saw as they did. From customer to Company to Jackson and back again, to understand Jackson is to understand more than the postcard business. Consider the following anecdotes. Think of them as parts of a parable:

Jackson became famous because of a single set of photographs he made while on assignment with Ferdinand Hayden's 1873 Geological Survey of the Rocky Mountains.

Hayden had recruited Jackson in 1870, soon after Jackson had set up a studio in Omaha, the railroad boom town of the Union Pacific. Jackson had begun there, on his own, by photographing Native Americans—Osages, Otoes, Pawnees, Winnebegoes, and Omahas —and selling their pictures to photo card companies back East. He struck it rich, as far as he was concerned, when he landed a contract with a New York stereo view company to photograph scenes along the route of the Union Pacific. This was a moment in the history of the West when there were still so many buffalo that a herd, moving through a mile-wide valley, could pack it, edge to edge, horizon to horizon as far as the eye could see.

In 1871, on assignment with Hayden's survey, Jackson took the first photographs ever published of Yellowstone—photographs used as evidence by Hayden (as well as by lobbyists for the Northern Pacific, who hoped to promote passenger travel on its route) to convince Congress to declare Yellowstone the nation's first National Park. Making these evidentiary photographs to honor and protect such a national monument gave Jackson his first public notice. His name became linked with easterners' conceptions of the West—its grandeur, its wondrous scale, its awesome— and unadulterated—beauty. Beyond that, Jackson's photographs authenticated Hayden's efforts. Congress authorized a bigger budget to carry the survey first into the Tetons and then into the Rockies.

In 1872, Jackson's wife died in child-birth. His baby daughter died soon after. By then, he'd sold his studio in Omaha, moved to Washington, D.C., and, as a government employee, headed back into the western mountains. In 1873, Hayden sent him into the Colorado Rockies on a picture-making itinerary that was to end with photographs of a western legend: the Mountain of the Holy Cross, a mountain said to have a deep crevice filled with snow, shaped like a huge cross, cut into the rock face of its summit. "No man we talked with," wrote Jackson, "had ever seen the Mountain of the Holy Cross, but everyone knew that somewhere in the far reaches of the western highlands such a wonder might exist. Hadn't a certain hunter once caught a glimpse of it—only to have it vanish as she approached? Didn't a wrinkled Indian...narrow his eyes and slowly nod when questioned? Wasn't this man's grandfather and that man's uncle and old so-and-so's brother the first white man to lay eyes on the Holy Cross—many, many, many years ago?"

The legend of the Cross of Snow had any number of variations: prospectors who saw it were said to have been cursed, jinxed, and died. Jackson was said to have been guid-ed by Chief Ouray, chief of the Uncompahgre Utes, a historical figure, but in Colorado the equivalent of Squanto, the Good Indian, who taught the Pilgrims how to grow corn. In fact, wrote Jackson, "anyone who wanted to see Holy Cross could climb Gray's Peak on a clear day and pick it up with field glasses. As one comes close to the cross, it always disappears behind Notch Mountain—and that is how the myth established itself." Hayden himself climbed Holy Cross with a party of surveyors to complete a triangulation from its summit. Jackson climbed Notch Mountain with his camera equipment, accompanied by the editor and publisher of Denver's *Rocky Mountain News*.

The photographs Jackson took made him renowned: they bore witness to the hand of God in nature; they revealed a sign—sure proof—of this country's Manifest Destiny. Europe—the Old World—might have its cathedrals, but America had its West, set aside for it by God since Creation.

Jackson's photographs inspired painters and poets. Longfellow, grieving the tragic death of his own wife, gazed from her portrait to a reproduction of Jackson's picture and wrote "The Cross of Snow," comparing himself to the mountain, his heart etched with sorrow. Variations of Jackson's image, in print and engraving, in oval format and stereograph, went through dozens of editions. Versions of it hung in parlors, in

parsonages, and in chapels. Nearly as soon as it was published in one of Hayden's reports, Jackson began to retouch: he opaqued the sky, then filled it with composited clouds; he extended and then enlarged the arms and body of the cross; he added a waterfall and a stream and turned a patch of ice into a "snow angel." No one accused him of fabrication. The cross was there and he had seen it—seen it and recorded it for all to see. Jackson became America's true witness.

Two events more or less coincided with the publication of Jackson's photographs:

First: a war party of Sioux killed six railway workers extending the line of the Northern Pacific into the Yellowstone Valley. A force of cavalry, led by George Armstrong Custer, was sent to clear the Black Hills of hostiles. Gold prospectors followed the troops. The prospectors dug holes in ground the Sioux held holy.

Second: the Credit Mobile Scandal caused a financial Panic. The vice president, the vice president elect, and any number of

senators and congressmen were discovered to have taken very large bribes from a railway-construction holding company run by directors of the Union Pacific. That holding company—the Credit Mobile—had skimmed a total of $50 million from Union Pacific construction contracts since the railroad's directors had established it—for their benefit—in 1867.

Because of the Panic, appropriations for the 1873–1874 survey were slow in coming. As soon as Hayden had the money, he dispatched Jackson to the Southwest. For the next several years, Jackson photographed cliff dwellings few white men had ever seen.

In 1876, at nearly the same moment the Sioux finally rubbed out Custer at Little Big Horn, the U.S. Centennial Exposition opened in Philadelphia. It was there that Alexander Graham Bell demonstrated his telephone, first to a small group of eminent men, then to the public. Hayden had given Jackson the job of building clay scale models of the cliff dwellings he'd photographed at Mesa

02905 MT OF THE HOLY CROSS.　　　　　　　　　　DETROIT PHOTOGRAPHIC CO

Verde in southwestern Colorado. "When the fair opened," wrote Jackson, "this display attracted more attention than the many photographs and all the rocks and relics of Dr. Hayden's career. It drew almost as many visitors as Dr. Alexander Graham Bell's unprobable [invention]."

Eighteen seventy-eight was the last year Jackson worked for the survey. On his way back from Wyoming, he visited Yellowstone. What he found dismayed him. "It was a park, indeed," he wrote, "with rangers and tourists—and a cavalry detachment to guard them from Indians!" Lodges had been built and riding trails laid out. Crowds gathered to watch the geysers; the sick "took the waters"; the healthy "bathed." Everywhere, rocks and mineral deposits had been broken off by souvenir hunters. With the help of Jackson's photographs, the Northern Pacific and the federal government had succeeded in turning a version of the Garden of Eden into a tourist attraction.

What happened next completes one parable about Jackson's early life:

In 1879, out of work and now married again—to the niece of Colorado's first governor and the daughter of the federal agent in charge of the Omaha Reservation—Jackson opened a studio in Denver, as frenzied a railway town as Omaha had ever been. In ten years—from 1870 to 1880—the city's population had grown from 5,000 to 35,000. One hundred settlers a day—prospectors and prostitutes, dreamers and dry goods salesmen, carpenters and coffin makers—arrived on their way to silver towns in the mountains. Every year, thousands of passengers and millions of tons of freight passed through the city's rail hub. By 1879, the city had two telephone systems; by 1884, it had an opera house, built by the Matchless Mine's Bonanza King, Horace Tabor, an old acquaintance of Jackson's. Based on what he knew and whom he knew, Jackson guessed that Denver would keep growing and he would grow with it. He

guessed right: "Denver's population tripled between 1880 and 1890," he later wrote, "and so did my income." As well known, well connected, and well positioned as he was, Jackson wanted more.

In the spring of 1879, he took a train to New York to ask Jay Gould for a favor. If there was ever an American Mephistopheles, it was Jason Gould.

Henry Adams, that genteel anti-Semite, believed Gould was a Jew, so stereotypically devious, greedy, and driven was he; but Adams was wrong. Poverty, frailty, and a failed Yankee farmer for a father had made Gould into a wretched but very bright little boy who dreamed of building his very own railroad across the continent "so that," he told his sister, "California might be closer to us."

Black haired, black bearded, dark eyed, and consumptive, Gould had made his first fortune fleecing Cornelius Vanderbilt of millions of dollars by selling him counterfeit Erie Railroad stock certificates that Gould and his partner, Jim Fisk, had printed.

By 1869, Gould had bribed President Grant's brother-in-law to spy on him while Gould cornered all the gold in circulation to drive up its price. When Grant discovered what was happening and ordered the Treasury to sell federal gold, the market crashed in the "Panic of Black Friday"— but not before Gould had sold what he owned for a profit of $11 million. With that, he bought control of the Union Pacific after the Credit Mobile Scandal had cut its price by two-thirds. Once in control, Gould bought a network of broken-down railway companies—the Detroit Pacific, the Wabash, the Missouri Pacific, and others—whose only value were tracks that ran parallel to the route of the Union Pacific. Once Gould owned them—worthless as they were, he used them to blackmail his own company, to buy them to prevent competition. Gould's "streaks of rust" netted him $10 million.

By the time Jackson came to New York to ask him for a favor, Gould controlled 10,000 miles of track throughout the Southwest and was poised to take control of the Western Union Telegraph Company. So powerful, hated, and pervasive was Gould's influence, so ruthless and manipulative were his tactics, and so extensive was his network of spies and agents that when, in 1885 and 1886, the rail workers of the Knights of Labor struck his Southwest System, they ignited a wildfire of strikes—culminating in the Haymarket bombing—that became one of the biggest and most bitter labor upheavals this country had ever known.

This was the man William Henry Jackson asked for a favor. Not much of one, either. Just a few letters recommending him as a photographer to the directors of the Denver Pacific and the Denver and Rio Grande, two of the railroads Gould owned. Wrote Jackson, "as I walked towards his desk, I felt as if I were being X-rayed by the blackest, most piercing eyes in the world.... Gould's name reeked, but he was king."

Gould was very polite and soft spoken. He remembered the stereo views Jackson had made, years before, of scenes along the route of the Union Pacific. The two men chatted about flowers. "Gould was an expert gardener," wrote Jackson, "and knew unmeasurably more than I ever would.... No doubt he was a cold and unscrupulous man. But he was extraordinarily intelligent and I have always found it hard to dislike any person gracious enough to show an interest in the things that concern me."

Gould wrote Jackson his letters. Every summer, for the next fifteen years, Jackson rode the Denver and Rio Grande—more often than not in the railway president's private rail car—taking pictures for the company along its route.

The question is: Why would anyone ask the Devil for a favor? In particular: Why would someone who'd taken photographs— and become famous for taking photographs —of God made manifest in nature, ask the Devil to write him a few recommendations? Even more to the point: Why would a man who'd seen with his own eyes what tourists, inspired by his photographs, had done to Yellstone—why would such a man want to take more photographs to inspire more people to take more vacations?

This is probably too judgmental. Jackson was no prophet. He was a commercial photographer; Gould was the boss of some potential clients. Why shouldn't Jackson have gone to the top and made his pitch? Railroads were wonderful. People like Thoreau may have had their doubts, and, certainly, railroads hadn't helped the buffalo or the Indians, but railroads were the lifeline of towns, cities, factories, and farms. Railroads made local economies, regional; regional economies, national. The market economy, ferocious and unregulated, may have made a few people very rich, a few more prosperous, and many more comfortable—and the rest sick, exhausted, and dead. But the same rail line that hauled ore and carried wheat also carried people to places like Yellowstone and the Grand Canyon so they could refresh themselves in the presence of the sublime. Of course, if people kept taking chunks of it home with them, there wouldn't be much left except some turnstiles and a few trash heaps.

Jackson made his deal with the Devil because he thought—like everyone else—that he'd come out ahead. Denver would grow and he'd grow with it. Fifteen years later, he discovered that he'd overextended himself—so much so that he had to rob Peter to pay Paul. To pay off business debts, he embezzled money from his mother-in-law, money entrusted to him to pay off mortgages on some building lots bought as speculative investments. To cover his tracks (to pay the interest on the mortgages he should have paid off), Jackson dipped into business receipts without telling his new partner. When the depression of 1893—which included the demonetization of silver—flattened Denver's economy, the risks Jackson had taken proved nearly fatal: the commercial studio he'd expanded and expanded and expanded suddenly had too few clients. The real estate in which he and his family had speculated was suddenly worth much less than what they'd paid for it.

Jackson's solution was as classically American as the mess he'd gotten into: he left town. In fact, he left the country. The agent of his salvation (which soon proved to be no salvation at all) was a publicist for the Baltimore and Ohio Railroad with the Dickensian name of Pangborn. If Jay Gould was Lucifer, then Joseph Gladding Pangborn was a little devil, a smooth talker who made himself comfortable by making his bosses look good.

Jackson made pictures for Pangborn along the route of the Baltimore and Ohio; Pangborn installed them quite handsomely—with William Henry Jackson, the famous photographer, in attendance—in the Transportation Pavilion of the World's Colombian Exposition in Chicago. So handsomely, in fact, that Pangborn talked his boss, Marshall Field, as well as some of his boss's friends—George Westinghouse, George Pullman, Cornelius Vanderbilt, Jr., and Andrew Carnegie—into financing a Transportation Commission that would tour the world to study and to acquaint the British in India and the Russians in Siberia with the wonderful things (steamships and trains) they might buy from America. Pangborn hired Jackson as Hayden had once hired him, to document and authenticate the undertaking. Eighteen months later, the commission ran out of money in Russia. By then it had visited, and Jackson had made photographs, in North Africa, Egypt, India, China, and Japan. It was in Japan that one member left the commission after he discovered that Pangborn had been embezzling his salary. Jackson made it back to New York as broke as he was when he'd left the country. That was when Edwin Husher found him and told him about the Detroit Publishing Company.

When Jackson asked Jay Gould for a favor, he was no Faust, he was just counting on progress to tip the scales in his favor. Progress evolved into a little man named Pangborn, and Pangborn nearly left Jackson stranded in Siberia. There may be a moral to this about progress, but there's something else as well. Jackson was as well acquainted with God as with the Devil. Knowledge of one impelled knowledge of the other.

William Jackson was born in a little town in upstate New York across the Hudson from Burlington. After doing nothing more dangerous in the Civil War than making sketches and guarding some baggage trains at Gettysburg, he went West. What he experienced there were vistas so grand and so extended, so massive and—compared to the East—so limitless, that to be in that landscape was to be like Melville's Pip, the cabin boy, thrown overboard and left, bobbing alone in the sea. Somehow or other, Jackson learned to reproduce the depth, breadth, and enormity of all that on flat pieces of glass coated with silver salts. The East was constricted toil and trouble, and the West was freedom; the East was a man-made tangle, and the West was a soaring release.

That's what Jackson's eye understood and encompassed: immense forms in immense space, seen from above, like an eagle in level flight, or a recording angel, going about his business. The mountains and cliffs and canyons of the West burned themselves into Jackson's brain, so that after all the tumble and jumble of Denver and the bitter folly of Mr. Pangborn and his commission, what Jackson saw when he came East again was something strangely recognizable. The new vistas in the new cities may have been manmade, but they were massive and grand, not equal to any mountain range or canyon, but close enough, so that from a proper height or from a proper distance, a camera could pay homage to them as if they were bluffs or buttes or mesas. In the West, such inhuman scale would have been humbling but transcendent; in the East, it was splendid but crushing: men might bow down before God, but they were dwarfed by their fellows. The great strength and suppleness of Jackson's eye was that, encountering one, he could recall the other. The images he made and the many he supervised had a wondrous—and disciplined—luxury of space to them, but, step to the left or step to the right, or come back to the same scene in the early evening, and what had been a cityscape inspired by Bierstadt might become a piazza painted by de Chirico. God and the Devil, golden dreams and no possibilities, free will and no freedom at all—Jackson understood both and encoded his hope in his images.

There's just a bit more to all this, and it's personal.

For ten years I looked at the images in the Detroit Collection and, for ten years, every time I saw them, I caught my breath. I couldn't quite understand why until first my father and then my mother died. No one in my father's village in Poland recorded his birth, but he believed he was born in December 1899. My mother had a certificate: she was born on a farm near Cleveland in 1903. They each lasted ninety-four years.

As I was working on this book, my mother went blind. She had her wits about

her, so once she understood she'd never see again, she stopped eating, and in ten days, she was dead. As I watched, she turned from an old woman into an old crone, so old and shrunken that she could have been carved in stone above a portal, or painted in a crowd at the edge of a Last Judgment. As I stared at her, it suddenly occurred to me that she had once been young—a girl, quick-witted and beautiful. That's when I realized why the pictures I'd been looking at made me catch my breath.

Everyone thinks—fools that we are—that the world didn't exist until we opened our eyes and saw it. Our glance gives birth to the world. Blink once, blink twice, and the world flickers into existence. Not "After me, the Deluge," but "Before me, Nothing."

Photographs deny this. They attest to a world that existed without us witnessing it. But, as they deny our illusions, they also preserve them. When we look at a photograph, we have an experience—an optical and neurological experience—in the present, of seeing the past. Living in the

now, we look at the then, and, for a millisecond, before we can resume disbelief, we experience that vanished world as if it were as present as our rods and cones. That's why I kept catching my breath: when my mother glanced at the world in 1910, she was old enough not just to look at it, but to see it and remember it. As I looked at these photographs, my eyes became hers, my eyes became in hers. She was as dying and dead as her world, but just as present. Like the sense memories traced in her brain, those photographs were no hallucinations. Hidden inside the crone was a girl, and inside the girl was everything she had seen, felt, and known. As I gazed into the photographs, I became the sentient creature my mother once was, and the photographs, once memories, became facts again. The world inside my mother rustled in the breeze. It had just made a deal with the Devil but figured time was on its side. Maybe it was. Who knows? Maybe it is. ⬝

PLATES

PLATES

BIBLIOGRAPHY

Hales, Peter B. *William Henry Jackson and the Transformation of the American Landscape*. Temple University Press, Philadelphia, 1988.

Hughes, Jim. *The Birth of a Century: Early Color Photographs of America*. Tauris Park Books, London, 1994.

Jackson, William Henry. *Time Exposure*. University of New Mexico Press, Albuquerque, New Mexico 1986.

Lowe, James C., and Ben Pappel. *Detroit Publishing Company Collectors Guide*. Deltologists of America, Newton Square, Pennsylvania, 1975.

Reade-Miller, Cynthia. *Main Street, USA, in Early Photographs*. Dover, New York, 1988.